THE WOUNDS OF JESUS

*For the sisters of the Community of the Holy Cross
whose devotion to the Cross of our Lord Jesus Christ
is a constant support and inspiration*

Resource pictures by Kirsten Rosslyn-Smith
for personal meditation or for use in Lent courses
based on this book are available at
www.stjohns-nottm.ac.uk, and may be downloaded.

*A Meditation on the
Crucified Saviour*

THE WOUNDS OF
JESUS

CHRISTINA BAXTER

FOREWORD *by the* ARCHBISHOP *of* CANTERBURY

ZONDERVAN™

GRAND RAPIDS, MICHIGAN 49530 USA

ZONDERVAN™

The Wounds of Jesus
Copyright © 2004 by Christina Baxter

Requests for information should be addressed to:
Zondervan, *Grand Rapids, Michigan 49530*

Library of Congress Cataloging-in-Publication Data

Baxter, Christina.
    The wounds of Jesus : a meditation on the crucified Saviour / Christina
Baxter. – 1st ed.
      p. cm.
    Includes bibliographical references.
    ISBN 0-310-25791-3
    1. Jesus Christ – Crucifixion – Meditations. I. Title.
BT450.B345 2005
232.96 – dc22

                                        2004020580

Interior design by Beth Shagene

Printed in Great Britain by Clays Ltd, St Ives plc

04 05 06 07 08 09 10 /❖ CLY/ 10 9 8 7 6 5 4 3 2 1

CONTENTS

ACKNOWLEDGEMENTS

To the staff and students of St John's College, Nottingham, for some study leave in which to write this book; to the staff of Tyndale House, Cambridge, who were kind enough to give me a desk where I could read and think, and to Margaret Pollard, whose kind friendship enabled me to have a place to stay whilst I was working on the manuscript.

FOREWORD BY THE ARCHBISHOP OF CANTERBURY

Strange as it may sound, we still sometimes forget that Jesus truly was a physical being. What he was as a material body was part of what God said, what God communicated, in his whole identity – not a bit of stage scenery or decoration, not just a background against which ideas are talked about.

Christina's meditations on the wounds of Christ direct us again and again to what is said in the physical concreteness of Jesus' body. She brings us very close to that body, so that we can listen to God's communication and find ourselves met and touched as bodily beings ourselves.

Meditation on the wounds of Jesus is an ancient custom in the Western Church, and here it finds a genuinely modern expression, fully sensitive to where twenty-first-century believers are. Biblical scholarship combines with pastoral acumen and personal testimony to produce a moving and involving book – one which will undoubtedly be welcomed by study groups and individuals as a searching resource for a Lent in which self-understanding and understanding of God may grow in step with each other as they should.

✝ Rowan Cantuar

Archbishop of Canterbury

INTRODUCTION

Some years ago I was asked to speak at an international Christian conference, and chose to focus on the cross of Christ. A person of some standing in the organization, and almost certainly my senior in age, approached me afterwards to say how refreshing it had been since in her experience she never heard any sermons on this subject except on Good Friday. That comment startled me a good deal. Many Christians do not attend a Good Friday service nowadays, because they are expected to be at their place of work. If this means that some, or perhaps most, Christians never learn about the cross, then they are being deprived of the heart of their faith.

This Lent book is intended to address that issue by offering readers the chance to consider the crucified Saviour in order to deepen our devotion, enrich our worship and strengthen our discipleship. I am sure that if that happens other aims will also be fulfilled: we will embolden our witness and want to extend our service to the world. For centuries, Christians have believed that meditating on Jesus is an essential way in which we can open ourselves to the transforming grace of his Spirit which enables us to become more like him.

Nonetheless, we need to realize, as the first followers of Jesus found, that standing at the foot of the cross of Jesus is no easy thing. I write this introduction on the feast of St Mary Magdalene, who was one such disciple. According to the Gospels, some of the men among Jesus' followers never made it to Golgotha, but his mother, some other women and the beloved disciple were there to witness for the world the suffering, the forgiveness and the death of the Lord and Giver of Life. Their testimony has been the heart of the gospel for all later generations. We praise the God who strengthened them to look upon their son, healer, friend and teacher as he suffered and died. There is no doubt that his was the greater suffering, but theirs was also incalculable. I pray that, as you read this book, you may receive God's similar strength so that you also can be witnesses in your turn.

Before you read any further you might like to pray this prayer – which could be a prayer to use before you read each section or chapter:

> Most merciful God,
> by your Spirit you strengthened your Son
> so that he was able to suffer for us;
> send your Spirit now,
> so that we may be strengthened
> to look upon him whom we have pierced,
> to receive all the benefits of his passion,
> and to offer ourselves wholly to your service,
> for his dear name's sake,
> Amen.

Many books have been written about the passion of Jesus, from all kinds of perspectives. Some look at a particular Gospel; others look at the last words of Jesus from the cross; some are deeply theoretical; others are deliberately practical. I have chosen to consider the wounds which Jesus bore for us, so that we may give our primary attention to

Jesus himself. I hope that, as we think on each of these wounds, we will deepen our understanding of the meaning of his suffering and the cross. You may feel that you have seen new perspectives and come to fresh understanding, but if you still find yourself perplexed and puzzled about what it all means and how it "works", this may also be a real engagement with the tremendous mystery upon which we are focusing. There is much in Scripture which enlightens us about these things, but the Lord God says, "my thoughts are not your thoughts, nor are your ways my ways" (Isaiah 55:8), so a deepening sense of wonder which we cannot always express in words may be a most appropriate response to this study.

The proclamation of Christ crucified on the cross was as puzzling to people in the first century as it is to us today. Their perplexity, as St Paul makes clear, was that anyone could think that the Messiah, the Son of God, would be allowed to suffer in this cruel way (see 1 Corinthians 1:18–25). The very idea was abhorrent. Any contemporary of St Paul, investigating the Christian faith, might well have thought that Christians were worshipping a person who justly suffered a humiliating death on the cross. Nowhere in Greek, Roman or Jewish ideas of God was there any hint of the notion that God or God's chosen one might be crucified. Christians, of course, were well aware of this: "Jesus . . . endured the cross, disregarding its shame. . ." (Hebrews 12:2). Somehow those who were familiar with Jewish traditions also needed to make sense of the saying in Deuteronomy 21:23 that "anyone hung on a tree is under God's curse". Believing, proclaiming and explaining how it could be that a person who had been tortured, disgraced and accursed was now to be acknowledged as Lord and Saviour presented the apostles with a significant task. In one way we could read the whole New Testament as their answer to this problem.

So let's begin by learning what everyone in the ancient world would already know – exactly what was involved in crucifixion. The term could be used to refer either to the nailing up on a tree or post of the body of someone who had already been executed, or to the execution of someone who was strung up alive. Sometimes people were impaled on an upright post, or they might be hung from it. We know that in the time of Jesus people were crucified in many brutal ways. The "cross" was not always the same shape, nor was the body always hung vertically.

Roman crucifixion generally followed flogging, which could itself kill. Where this was not done, death was a very slow and extremely painful process extending over days, since the act of crucifixion alone did not touch any of the vital organs which would normally signal swift death. Generally the victim carried the crossbeam to the place of execution (not the whole cross including the upright pole, as Christian art often depicts). There the person was either nailed or lashed to the crossbeam. Nailing was not universal; people could be lashed to the cross at hands and feet – which extended the period of their slow death, partly caused by thirst, dehydration and hunger. Once they were fixed to the crossbeam, it was raised to the upright position using two Y-shaped props. Sometimes there was a notch in the top of the upright post into which the crossbeam was dropped, so that the cross was in fact T-shaped. At other times the notch was partway down the upright, so the upright post continued above the head of the crucified. This seems to be indicated in the case of Jesus, since they nailed the accusations above him (see Matthew 27:37; cf. Luke 23:38).

Occasionally a cross was so low that animals could attack the feet or lower part of the torso, but it is thought that the cross of Jesus would have been about seven feet high. Two concessions were sometimes made to the sufferer: there could be a small wooden peg or ledge upon which the buttocks were "seated", and/or a small platform for the feet to rest or press upon. Both of these took the weight of the body, though there is also evidence that the weight was taken by the wounds of the nails. These supports also made it less likely that the person would be able to wrench free of the cross while writhing in pain, since the body had a little more buttressing than that afforded by securing the hands and feet alone.

In cases where there was no support for the feet or the buttocks, those crucified either had to allow their whole body's weight to rest on the nailed or lashed feet, which was excruciatingly painful, or had to raise their body's weight to be carried in part by their nailed or lashed arms. Both positions were agonizing, but in the first position breathing would be extremely difficult, since exhalation was impossible, so in the end death probably came by asphyxiation. It is also suggested that breathing difficulties would follow the inevitable circulation problems caused by such brutal treatment, but it is impossible to know for certain what exactly was the usual final physical cause of death. There is little agreement amongst modern medical experts.

There were many wicked variations by which victims were tortured as they died, and the sight would be familiar enough to those hearing the preaching of the cross during the time of the early Church or reading any of the New Testament documents soon after they were written. For them, only the simplest detail needed to be given. In those times there was no need for imagination or films to fill in the story. There were mass crucifixions after insurrections – thousands killed at once. Everyone knew that it was normally a very bloody and excruciating death. It was regarded as the worst form of execution, reserved for the worst of criminals. It was utterly cruel and demeaning. So terrible was it that it was used only on the lowest classes of society and for the most heinous crimes such as treachery or treason. Moreover, it was believed to be such an effective deterrent that it was always carried out publicly, which enhanced the humiliation for those so punished. Often there was no permission given for burial, and the bodies suffered the same end as the countless animals slaughtered today at the side of the road – they were eaten by wild animals and birds. This was regarded as the final indignity.

Now that we have a basic idea of what crucifixion is like, I need to explain how I have structured this book. In each chapter I am going to explore the way that the cross hung over all we read about in the Gospels. This will help us to understand that one of the reasons why our Lord was able to endure the cross on Good Friday was that his whole life was cruciform, shaped by the cross to which he was journeying. He is able to call us to carry our cross and follow him every day because he himself had this daily discipline in Bethlehem, Nazareth and Galilee before he reached Jerusalem. His whole life had been a preparation for these hours. He does not ask us to do what he has not himself lived out.

Let me take one example. The New Testament suggests to us that when the Son of God became incarnate and was born as a truly human baby, there was already a self-emptying which made that condescension by God to our world possible. St Paul writes:

> Christ Jesus,
> who, though he was in the form of God,
> did not regard equality with God
> as something to be exploited,
> but emptied himself,
> taking the form of a slave,
> being born in human likeness. . .
>
> (Philippians 2:5–7)

Paul may himself have been quoting from an early Christian hymn with which he was familiar. Our own hymns also express this:

> In the bleak mid-winter
> A stable-place sufficed
> The Lord God Almighty,
> Jesus Christ.
>
> (Christina Rossetti, 1875)

I do not think we can claim that leaving the glory of heaven to become human was equal to the suffering and self-abasement of the cross, but we can certainly say that in this very act of entering our world the Son of God has shown us that his life of love is most truly expressed in letting go of power and status, for the sake of those he loves. And, of course, the chief reason why he became human was so that he could die for us and for our sins: "For the Son of Man came not to be served but to serve, and to give his life a ransom for many" (Mark 10:45). In a debate a few years ago, some hard questions were posed to the Church by one of its leaders as to what kind of God allowed the miracle of virginal conception or incarnation but did not also perform miracles to save the hundreds of people dying in the world's latest disasters. I think there would be no answer to that challenge if it were not the case that the miracles accompanying the birth of Jesus Christ occurred in order to enable God himself to suffer death to save us.

We sometimes speak of indications in early life that a person will be a great thinker or musician; we might properly speak of this child carrying indications from the very beginning of his life that he is to experience in adulthood the utter stripping of personal security, indeed of life itself, culminating in crucifixion. Although we do not see all the details of this through the ordinary development of the child and teenager in the "hidden years" which the Gospel writers do not record for us, we certainly begin to glimpse it once we read the Gospel narratives of opposition (Mark 1:21–3:6) and actual threats to his life, present from the very beginning of his public ministry according to Luke (4:16–30, especially verses 28–29). There is a sense in which the shadow of the cross is cast backwards into the daily routine of Jesus' life, because he began to embrace it as a child in the manger. Sometimes this is hinted at in Christian art, where the child of light lies on his back in the dark manger with arms outstretched so that the little form is in the shape of the cross towards which he is growing.

The call to carry our cross will not be easy – scholars have made it clear by their research that it would have been an unwelcome, even offensive, call to the people of the first century. To those upper classes who were usually exempt from crucifixion and to those slaves and other marginal peoples peculiarly vulnerable to it in daily life, the call to walk the way of the cross would have been particularly unattractive. They would have recent and horrific experience of what crucifixion meant in real life which would make this call – even if they understood that Jesus was using it as an analogy – a hard invitation to accept.

There will be opportunities to think and pray as you read, but this is also a practical book. God does want deep thinkers, but he also wants lives changed so that we can be people through whom he can establish and extend his kingdom. If the whole of Jesus' life is marked by the cross, we need to explore what it might mean for us to live lives which are also marked by the cross. That, after all, is what thousands of Christians claim they are committed to, as they are signed with a cross at baptism, as they wear a cross, carry a cross, or set up a cross in their homes. I believe that the struggle to understand how God, in Christ, was reconciling the world to himself (2 Corinthians 5:19) will need to be matched by another struggle: to discover how we can radiate the grace of God through our cruciform lives.

In each chapter you will find that I have given you seven sections to read – so that, if you are not able to read a whole chapter at a sitting, you could take these sections as daily readings for Lent. There will be a chance to do some Bible study in the first two sections of each chapter, and I will be using the New Revised Standard Version of the Bible. The pattern of each chapter is the same:

1 I will first help you to focus on that **part of Jesus' body** which will be wounded at the end of his life.

2 I will then explore the **wound which Jesus received** in his passion.

3 We will then look at this wound in relation to one of the **major episodes or themes of Jesus' life**, as a way of understanding that his death is a fulfilment and not a negation of the life he had lived up to that point.

4 We will then consider **the implications for us in the community of faith** to which we belong, and think

about what we might be called to do in the Church or in the world. I have tried to be imaginative in choosing my illustrations, but inevitably some will not be appropriate for your situation. Don't let that be an excuse to do nothing! Where my illustrations fail you, ask God to show you the equivalent in your time and place. I am hoping that you will be able to share your explorations with other Christians through a Lent group, so some of the ideas are specifically for such sessions. If your church or fellowship does not have a Lent group, why not start one? This could be the moment to invite your neighbours or the people with whom you spend your work or leisure time to join a group. You do not always have to work through your church structures.

5 There is then an opportunity to think about **what this might mean for us personally** in a section which you might want to make the topic for a meditation. You will find that I have taken some perspectives from St Patrick's Breastplate:

> Christ be with me, Christ within me,
> Christ behind me, Christ before me,
> Christ beside me, Christ to win me . . . etc.

6 Each chapter has a **conclusion**, which will draw the threads together and help you to sum up what you have been learning.

7 Finally I have included **questions to consider**, ideas for action and suggestions for group work.

The book has six chapters, each exploring the different wounds of Jesus – his back, feet, hands, side, head and heart. There are various traditions as to how many wounds Jesus experienced and how they are grouped together. Some Christians came to believe that there were five wounds – (1) head, (2 and 3) hands, (4) side, which includes his heart, and (5) feet. It seems that they counted his hands as two but his feet as one, since the feet were usually depicted as nailed together one over the other. I do not think, however, that we need to spend time wondering how to number the wounds. They were innumerable, through the scourging he received before he reached the cross. In popular devotion the five classic wounds were regarded as the guarantors of our five senses and were appealed to in prayers which began, "By your wounded hands. . ." and then added some petition against sin. There does not seem to be much writing about the wounds of Jesus in the early centuries of the Christian era, but in medieval times the widespread use of the crucifix and reports of saints receiving the stigmata changed that. One medieval prayer asks, "Let the five wounds of Christ be my medicine," and in Germany the wounds were referred to as "signs of love".[1]

This may not be an easy read; indeed, this may be a tough Lent! I know that when I take a three-hour service on Good Friday it always leaves me emotionally and physically exhausted. Standing by the cross is immensely hard work. When we see suffering we prefer to "do something about it", which is why it is so hard to accompany the suffering of the long-term sick or dying as we feel utterly helpless. But feeling utterly helpless is exactly where we need to be when we stand by the cross of Jesus. The New Testament makes it clear to us that we *are* utterly helpless – although we find that hard to hear and harder still to believe. "For while we were still weak, at the right time Christ died for the ungodly" (Romans 5:6). On the cross Jesus does for us what we cannot do for ourselves. How this happens and what he calls us to do about it is the subject of this book.

It is only when we realize that "nothing in my hand I bring; simply to thy cross I cling", that we can begin to apprehend all "the benefits of his passion" which he graciously bestows on his people. To help you keep this in mind through Lent you may wish to find a "holding cross" which is small enough to slip into your pocket. These are usually made of wood, shaped so that your hand can grasp it easily. Many Christian bookshops and retreat houses have them, and they are a good way to remind yourself what you are making the centre of your attention for these forty days. Instead of waiting with increasing frustration in the bus or checkout queue, you can close your hand round the cross and remind yourself of Jesus' patient endurance and his love for you and for the whole world, or you can continue to offer your own life as a sacrifice of joy to the one who has offered all for you. You do not need to use words to make this kind of prayer. The Lord knows your intentions. You may find this so helpful that it becomes a habit for the rest of your life and not just for Lent.

My prayer for you is that this Lenten study may help you to understand the "breadth and length and height and depth" of Jesus' love (Ephesians 3:18).

FOR FURTHER READING

Martin Hengel, *Crucifixion*, London: SCM Press, 1977.

Gerard S. Loyan, *The Crucifixion of Jesus: History, Myth, Faith*, Minneapolis: Augsburg Fortress Press, 1995.

1

HIS BACK
Baptism and Crucifixion

His body

The back to follow

You may never have thought of the back of Jesus before – and you have probably not heard a sermon about it either. So bear with me as I begin this chapter with some general reflections. Those who followed Jesus around Galilee were no doubt very familiar with his back. He strode ahead of the crowd, up the mountain or into the boat so that he could teach them. It is not always the case that we can recognize someone from the back – we are more accustomed to knowing people by their faces; but if people are well known to us we *can* recognize them from a distance by their characteristic posture. It might have been thus with Jesus. Although the New Testament does not say that he was a carpenter, it is likely that he learned his adoptive human father's trade, and he would therefore have developed strong shoulders and leg muscles from the hefty work of handling large pieces of wood. Carpenters in those times did not produce little figurines or dainty pieces; they built houses with wooden frames and did the whole work from felling trees to finishing doorposts. So this was a young man whose straight and strong back many learned to recognize.

The back turned on sin

Usually it was a back which the disciples followed willingly, but occasionally it was a back they did not want to see. Jesus turned his back on Peter when he tried to tempt him to avoid the cross, saying, "Get behind me, Satan!" (Mark 8:33). And he may well have turned his back on other temptations. We know that he had learned how to resist them from his mother, whose gentle schooling laid the foundations for his resistance to Satan in the desert.

The back to watch

It is likely that the disciples watched the back of Jesus in Gethsemane, for as long as they could stay awake. In this Gospel story (Mark 14:32–42) we see Jesus trembling on the brink of abandoning the path of obedience upon which he had embarked after struggling with the temptations in the wilderness – trembling on the brink of abandoning the work of bringing in God's kingdom in the way that he had been preaching to others. Here we see him longing and praying that God would not bring him to the time of trial, just as he had taught the disciples to pray for such protection (Luke 11:4). We see him wrestling with profound questions: Have I really got to drink this cup of suffering? Have I really got to be king of this kingdom, crowned with thorns? And so he walked a little way from the disciples and, falling on the ground, prayed ardently and desperately, "Abba, Father, for you all things are possible; remove this cup from me; yet, not what I want, but what you want" (Mark 14:36).

It is interesting, isn't it, that at the moment when there is most despair, most temptation to disobey, most cause for extreme anxiety, Jesus speaks in the most intimate way to God: Abba, Father. To address God in this familiar way was almost certainly highly unusual for the time – which is probably why the listening disciples remembered it. Jesus knew that God was his Abba Father: had God not said so at the beginning? "You are my Son, the Beloved," he said at Jesus' baptism, and again at the transfiguration (Mark 1:11; cf. 9:7). Perhaps when the temptations, so fierce at the beginning of his ministry, returned again at this critical final phase, Jesus' memory leapt back to the revelation which had impelled him into the wilderness combat, when the Father had assured him of his Sonship. Maybe that is why now, at the moment of his greatest trial, with his back turned to his disciples, Jesus ventures to address God as "Abba, Father" as he begins his prayer that it might be otherwise.

And isn't it odd that there is no reply? No word from heaven this time, no word of assurance or encouragement. No voice saying, "This *is* the right way." The answer to Jesus' prayer is the relentless march of events – and Jesus clearly takes that as affirmation that he must, after all, drink this cup. Perhaps it is not too surprising that, as Jesus is launched unanswered into the events of the passion, he turns to the words of a psalm and later cries out as he hangs dying, "My God, my God, why have you forsaken me?" (Mark 15:34).

In Gethsemane, there being no reply to his prayer, Jesus turns back to the three disciples who are nearest to him. And there he finds them, the mirror image of God himself – silent, apparently taking no notice at all. They are asleep. How could they fall asleep at this moment, the night so special, the events so tense? How could they fall asleep? In that moment Jesus must have felt entirely alone.

The silence of God which Mark implies is modified a little in Luke's account, where "an angel from heaven appeared to him and gave him strength" (Luke 22:43). For

Luke, the outcome of the prayer is the same as for Mark: Jesus will need to embrace his vocation to suffer, but there is divine preparation which this thoroughly human person receives. The strengthening comes not from the Word who is incarnate, whom we also know as the divine Son of God, for this divine person has been so united with the historical human Jesus that the human anguish is the Son's anguish. The one Lord Jesus Christ, both divine and human, receives the divine strengthening of the Father by the Spirit, which we are to presume the angel ministers to him, in both his divine and his human natures, as he kneels before the disciples.

When we read Luke's narrative, we can assume that it is only once the strengthening has occurred that Jesus is ready to pray for himself that he may endure the trials rather than be saved from them.

- With great urgency, he bids the disciples pray for themselves. He understands far better than they how vulnerable they will be once he has been arrested and executed. They need to pray the prayer he has taught them with much fervency: "Do not bring us to the time of trial" (Luke 11:4). He says to Peter, "Simon, are you asleep? Could you not keep awake one hour? Keep awake and pray that you may not come into the time of trial" (Mark 14:37–38).

- Jesus is inviting them to join the prayer he himself is praying for them. He has already prayed for their protection, as he indicates both to Peter personally ("Simon, Simon, listen! Satan has demanded to sift all of you like wheat, but I have prayed for you that your own faith may not fail; and you, when once you have turned back, strengthen your brothers"

[Luke 22:31–32]) and to all the disciples ("Father . . . I am asking on their behalf . . . Holy Father, protect them in your name . . . I am not asking you to take them out of the world, but I ask you to protect them from the evil one" [John 17:1, 9, 11, 15]).

• So what is it that the disciples are asked to do? Watch and pray that they may not enter into the time of trial. If they had watched Jesus, they would have seen not only a person who was in utter distress, struggling with the will of God, but someone who at that moment was able to be concerned about others, someone who at that moment opened up the possibility for them to receive the grace of God they so badly needed. If Jesus is going to endure the cross, they are also facing their hour of temptation or trial as they stand beside him or run away; as they stay at the foot of the cross or flee to some "safe" place. And so they find that Jesus invites them to open themselves to God, to receive his strengthening grace and mercy which alone will enable them to be faithful to the end. They find that Jesus, who is himself struggling with the suffering he is to endure, is also the one who points them to the divine resources they will need to support them through their own forthcoming trials.

I believe we may conclude that, while it might be the case that Jesus took the disciples with him for human company at his hour of need, it is also the case that even here, in his vulnerability, he offered them the chance to be disciples – to see how to discern the will of the Father, how to pray honestly, how to endure suffering, how to encourage others while facing the gravest trial yourself. All these lessons were being offered as they watched, for a while at least, his most holy back, which would soon be wounded for their transgressions.

His wounds

This back, then, was subject to the cruel flogging which was part of Jesus' physical suffering for us. Flogging in the ancient world was a brutal affair, and some victims died from that alone. Normally the victim was stripped, and thrown to the ground or bound to a low post or pillar. Occasionally the flogging took place as a condemned man carried the crossbeam to his place of execution. There seems to have been a number of instruments of torture, and they may have used different ones for different kinds of prisoners. Some suggest that rods were used on those who were free, sticks on soldiers and scourges on others. Scourges were generally leather thongs fitted with pieces of bone or lead or with spikes. These were the weapons which caused most damage. The various terms, "beating", "flogging", "scourging" and so on, might indicate different sentences or degrees of punishment, but it is difficult to know whether any such distinctions held at the time of Jesus. There seems, however, to have been a custom of flogging condemned prisoners before they were crucified in order to shorten the suffering on the cross.

Jesus' flogging or scourging is recorded for us in all the Gospels except Luke, although the point at which it comes in the Gospel narratives differs. In John it takes place during the questioning, and in Mark, followed by Matthew, it comes at the end of the "trial". We will look at both these accounts.

Flogging to interrogate and placate

"Then Pilate took Jesus and had him flogged" (John 19:1). Early in the morning Jesus was taken, bound, from the questioning before the Jewish authorities to the headquarters of Pilate, who was reluctant to try him ("Take him yourselves and judge him according to your law" [John 18:31]) and equally reluctant eventually to condemn him ("Look, I am bringing him out to you to let you know that I find no case against him" [John 19:4]).

Preliminary questions produced no certain outcome (John 18:33–38), so Pilate offered to release Jesus as the customary Passover act of leniency. When this was peremptorily refused, Pilate "took Jesus and had him flogged" (19:1), hoping that when his accusers saw that Jesus had already suffered physical torture and public ignominy, they would relent in their calls for the death sentence, clearing the way for Pilate to release him. Contemporary records suggest that Pilate was violent and self-willed but the political situation was volatile, so he had other factors to consider beyond the question of justice. The Passover season heightened this, because Jerusalem was full of pilgrims, when a Roman governor would least be able to take the risk of inflaming relations between the occupying power and the resentful subject nation.

After the flogging, some of the soldiers took liberties with the prisoner, dressing him up and mocking him. Pilate then presented the severely abused Jesus to his enemies, but the desire for the death penalty was by no means diminished. Eventually there were more legal interrogations and Pilate caved in to the insistence of the accusers. The description suggests that this flogging happened inside the praetorium, since Jesus is described as going in (John 18:33) and being brought out afterwards (19:4).

The final scourging

"After flogging Jesus, he [Pilate] handed him over to be crucified" (Matthew 27:26; cf. Mark 15:15). In this narrative the flogging is assumed to be part of the death sentence and happens after Pilate has given his final decision. The text here also seems to be describing the crueller scourging. If we are right to read the two narratives of flogging found in the Gospels together (i.e. John and Matthew-Mark), we may suppose that Jesus endured two floggings. If that was indeed the case, then it is no wonder that he did not hang on the cross long before he died. But we need to remember that this is conjecture, since all three of these Gospels only mention one flogging each, even though they suggest that it happened at different points in the "trial".

The crossbeam – raw wounds against rough wood

All the Gospels describe this event, although John does not mention the need to press Simon of Cyrene into service to carry the crossbeam for Jesus. As I mentioned earlier, the vertical part of the cross was normally permanently erected, while the horizontal part was carried by the condemned person. "Often it was carried behind the nape of the neck like a yoke, with the condemned's arms pulled back and hooked over it."[1] Although it was not usual for a condemned person to have the crossbeam carried by another, the Roman soldiers did not act out of pity. If Jesus was already so weakened by possibly two floggings, they needed to get him to the place of execution so that their orders to crucify him could be carried out before he died of other causes.

We cannot imagine what it was like for someone who had, in the course of his work, often carried heavy pieces of wood on his shoulders now to have thrust upon him a roughly hewn plank or tree which cut into every exposed wound. St Bernard of Clairvaux is believed to have received a prayer from the Lord which focused on this moment in his passion. Bernard prayed:

> O loving Jesus . . . I salute and worship the most sacred wound on your shoulder on which you carried the heavy cross, which so tore your flesh and laid bare your bones as to inflict on you an anguish greater than any other wound of your most blessed body.

Whether this was indeed the most painful of the wounds we will never know in this life, but when I was thinking in detail about Jesus' wounds his back (including his shoulder) seemed to me to warrant a chapter of its own.

Having carried the heavy crossbeam to the place of their execution, victims were then usually nailed to the beam before being hung up to die. Sometimes their arms were also lashed to prevent any escape. In the National Gallery in London there is a painting by Gerard David (active 1484; died 1523) which depicts this very act, showing the soldiers nailing the prone Saviour to the cross. Jesus' face depicts horror and shock; it stares at the viewer in such a way that I find it hard to contemplate for any length of time. Harder still, I find, is the effort required to imagine "what pain he had to bear".

His life – baptism and crucifixion

How did the life of Jesus prepare him to suffer the flogging, the bearing of the crossbeam and the torturous hanging with his deeply scarred back thrust against the cruel wood of the cross?

He learned to turn his back on his former way of life at his baptism; not in the sense that we turn our back on our former sinful way of life at our baptism, for, as John the Baptist pointed out to him, there was no formal need for him to be baptized for his own sake. When Jesus came to be baptized, "John would have prevented him, saying, 'I need to be baptized by you, and do you come to me?' But Jesus answered him, 'Let it be so now; for it is proper for us in this way to fulfil all righteousness'" (Matthew 3:14–15). So Jesus did come consciously to John, knowing that whatever might have gone before, the comfort and steady rhythm of life in his home town, with the working of wood and the people who had known him since childhood, had now come to an end. As there had been conscious abandonment of the place of glory at the moment of incarnation, there was now abandonment of the place of safety – his home, where there had been regular meals to eat, a pattern of prayer and worship with his contemporaries, and the support of his mother and extended family. He knew he was to leave all that now. "Jesus said . . . 'Foxes have holes, and birds of the air have nests; but the Son of Man has nowhere to lay his head'" (Matthew 8:20). And as he prepared to turn his back on what most of us value so highly, so the shadow of the cross became clear in his life. Once he had been baptized, he became increasingly certain that there would be no going back to the daily routine. Indeed, so "irregular" did his life become that even his family came to question his sanity – "they went out to restrain him, for people were saying, 'He has gone out of his mind'" (Mark 3:21).

And so Jesus came to John. Here he heard the fiery preaching – "You brood of vipers! Who warned you to flee from the wrath to come?" (Luke 3:7) – and resolved to identify himself completely with the radical way of life which God called for through his prophet. He overruled John's godly reluctance, in order to "fulfil all righteousness". This has been understood in many ways, at least two of which will help us to recognize Jesus' actions here as part of the preparation for the suffering he would experience at his flogging.

Preparing to shoulder our sins

First, Jesus identifies completely with his fellow human beings. He does not try to stand aside at this point as if he were only divine, with no need of repentance, or as if his main purpose in life is to protect his innocence and sinlessness. If God is calling people to repentance, then Jesus will go with them to repentance. This has helped the Church in its later reflections to see that Jesus' identification with us was part of his doing for us what we could not do for ourselves. Even our repentance is not as God would have it; our motives are always so mixed and our understanding of sin so partial.

Secondly, therefore, Jesus repents on behalf of his people. Where we are half-blinded about what is wrong, and often half-hearted about repenting and reluctant to put things right, he will repent thoroughly and completely on our behalf, seeing and naming our faults for what they are. Where we have settled into our habitual sinfulness, which has taken on a comfortable familiarity, he will repent for us of our collusion with wrongdoing and our reaping of its benefits.

When we repent, we ask God to see the repentance of Jesus and make that ours; when we try to put our lives right, we ask God to send us the Spirit of Jesus so that we have a new vision to see things as he sees them, and a new desire to change. In his repentance and baptism at the Jordan, Jesus begins to shoulder our sins and to make them his responsibility. In submitting to baptism, he thus begins the process which will lead him on to stand in our place as he is falsely accused and flogged for wrongdoing which is not his own, but which he carries for us.

What does this mean for us as a faith community?

The cross behind us

At this early stage of our study, we need to explore something of what it means to believe that in the cross the Lord Jesus Christ has carried on his back and has dealt with the sins of the whole world. "He himself bore our sins in his body on the cross, so that, free from sins, we might live for righteousness. . ." (1 Peter 2:24). There are some particular consequences of this of which we are not always aware. For instance, if the death of Jesus is sufficient for the sins of all, then that includes communal sin as well as the individual sin upon which Western Christians so often focus. This surely means that as well as confessing our personal sins, trusting that God will forgive for Christ's sake, we also need to be conscious of the sins of the communities to which we belong. We may not be the ones who have made the decisions which have brought us to the current difficulties, but we cannot wash our hands of the fact that we belong to these communities and therefore these things have been done in our name.

Two examples of this may enable you to think of the things in which you are embroiled, wittingly or unwittingly.

The first is the alleged atrocities against prisoners committed by the armed forces of North America and the United Kingdom in Iraq following the formal end of the war. Most of you reading this book may not have been aware of such activities until the media published the allegations. Yet those directly responsible have been acting in our name – if we belong to these nations. We can confess to God that we believe anything of this kind which may have been done is contrary to his expressed will (e.g. in the command to love your neighbour as yourself, Luke 10:27) and that we repent on behalf of our nation for what has happened. Then we can pray for the victims and their families, and for the perpetrators – true repentance which will involve a change of attitude and a change of lifestyle.

The second example is closer to home. It may be the case that our local community is so careless of the vulnerable – whether elderly or young – that someone dies alone and remains undiscovered for weeks, or a young child is abducted. Again, it may not be in our street, and it may not be something which we personally could have prevented. Nonetheless, we can confess to God that we are sorry we have consented to our society being ordered in such a way that these people have not had the protection they deserved, and we can ask God to forgive us and our community before we consider what we might do to ensure that history does not repeat itself. The least we might do is to pray for the vulnerable in our community, and to write with our concerns to our democratic representatives, our local councillors or Member of Parliament. But there may be other, more constructive things which we could initiate or with which we could assist.

These "little things" matter because sin (however unintentional) left untended spreads like wildfire and a culture grows up in which people accept as normal what should be regarded as morally abnormal or abhorrent. Our prayers can be used by God like the ring of burnt earth which fire-fighters clear to prevent the flames of a bushfire jumping from one area to another. Nothing which I have written is intended to suggest that our praying can ensure God's for-giveness of another individual – our prayers for the indi-viduals who might bear responsibility must be that they will come to see their actions as God sees them, and seek his forgiveness in Jesus Christ. But I do believe that the effects of those sins in individual or community life can be "contained" by our decision to shoulder our little part of the responsibility and confess our shame and sorrow to God, before we move on to more positive actions.[2]

Exactly the same principle applies to the life of the church community to which we belong. When things go wrong (and they seem to do so very frequently in the church communities I know), it is easy to distance ourselves from the trouble. Much like the Pharisee of the parable (Luke 18:11), we thank God that it was not us or our group who initiated the trouble, overlooking sometimes that our silence, or our willingness to listen to gossip without raising questions, has allowed the grumble or rebellion to grow.

An understanding of the call to carry the cross, however, implies for us that we do not try to shift away from respon-sibility. Instead we are to share that responsibility with those who may be nearer the centre of the problem, or even carry it for them in confessing with them and in part for them the wrongs that have been done. So we should say, "We have hurt one another," rather than, "Your group has hurt our group." We should confess, "We have not loved one another, and we ask God's forgiveness of us all." In carrying our sins to the cross, Jesus dealt with those things we could not handle ourselves. Now he invites us, as part of our own cross-carrying, not to try to justify ourselves – there is no need for that, we have been "justified by faith" (Romans 5:1) – but to learn by his example to be the friend of sinners. He alone could be the sinless friend of sinners; we must learn to be the sinful friend of sinners, standing alongside others in equal need of grace, praying for ourselves and others that we may receive the gift of repentance, and for ourselves and others that we may receive the gift of forgiveness.

On occasions it may be important that the community as a whole prays these prayers of corporate repentance in public, as a way of addressing issues which too often in our churches and society are left unnamed and unattended. For instance, if our local church has "squeezed out" some groups – perhaps teenagers, or ethnic groups – then, when we have been brought to recognize our own wrongdoing, we need to acknowledge that our attitudes have been wrong and to confess them in a formal prayer or liturgy. It is certainly something which we have started to do at St John's (the college where I teach, which I regard as something of a laboratory of experimental theology), so that we all learn how to respond to God's grace. We have found it to be an important part of how we live together.

Carrying the burdens of others

As we watch, in our mind's eye, the progress of Jesus along the *via dolorosa*, the way of sorrows, struggling to carry the crossbeam on a back already bleeding and covered in open sores from the flogging, we hear again his call to carry our cross. What might it mean for us as a Christian community to carry the burdens of others when they cannot bear the weight themselves? It seems to me that our carrying of others' burdens will shape our lives, as it shaped the life of Jesus. The Japanese theologian Kosuke Koyama, in a book called *No Handle on the Cross*, writes, "A man does not carry a cross as he carries his briefcase." That is a comment to ponder deeply. I take him to be pointing out to us that there is no convenient way to be a Christian or to belong to a Christian community. If we take the gospel seriously, it will in the end shape all that we are and do – just as it bowed Jesus to the ground with the effort of completing his saving work.

What would happen to our church life if we were in any way corporately to carry the burdens of those around us? We in the West have countless lessons to learn from African and Asian Christians who instinctively do this, faced with atrocities which we can only imagine. I will offer just one example here, but I know of many more. In Uganda, the "Lord's Resistance Army" terrorizes people in the area of Teso and they are forced to flee for their lives into safer areas. There they find that the churches and their leaders are willing to carry their refugee neighbours' burdens as they share their little material possessions and food with those in desperate need. Many Christians from other parts of the world also "carry this cross" as they share their resources to offer emergency help or regular support.

Some churches have a long and good heritage of carrying the burdens of others closer to home, in the places where they live. The work of the Salvation Army is a fine example. In many local Anglican churches, however, there is a real reluctance to engage with these issues except at arm's length through outside agencies. These churches seem to think that their congregational numbers are too few to make a difference, and the age range (too young or too old) is often not such as to enable much hands-on relief.

We need to remember two things. We are called to carry the burdens of others (Galatians 6:2), so the simple practical part of our imitation of Christ is not optional for any mobile Christian individual. At the same time, however, we are called into his body, the Church, so we need to think about what we can do *together*. Some things are much better done by a group of Christians acting together. We should not think only of the local worshipping community where we may find ourselves, but also of the larger group of churches which may make up the Christian fellowship in a town or city. So, for example, in Nottingham one larger church may be able to organize a soup run or a feeding programme, but all the churches working together may be able to do something far more constructive to meet the needs of the homeless, perhaps by offering hostel accommodation and other support.

When we think of ourselves as part of the body of Christ, we can recognize that we may have an occasional part to play – perhaps on a monthly rota, or that we have a part to play at some stages of our lives – when we are early retired, or before we are married and have children. An individual's part may simply be to pray and give towards the work, but there are usually social needs in which we can help occasionally if not regularly. So we need to think about our participation in this ecclesiologically – in the context of the wider Church, and eschatologically – in the context of the end times. While Church history is sometimes written as if there were great Christians who single-handedly changed the shape of a society, the truth is that even where there were great leaders, for instance in the movement to halt the slave trade, they were dependent on the collaboration and support of others who enabled them to play a leading role. Even Jesus needed the assistance of

Simon of Cyrene to enable him to reach Golgotha, and it is not too much to guess that the little group at the foot of the cross prayed for him in his anguish (John 19:25). At the end time, when all the secrets of people's hearts and lives will be laid bare, we will see that although it may be the case that the central figures played a crucial role in carrying the burdens of those who were bowed down in their societies, the supporting parts of their contemporaries were crucial in the final outcomes which we applaud. Our attitudes, encouragement, prayers, giving and political protests may not seem much at the time, but they may be the essential contributions which make possible the larger carrying or relief of people's burdens.

What does this mean for us personally?

Watching as we are bidden – for our own sake

I am basing this section on a series of meditations in which I entered imaginatively into the experience of the three disciples sitting in Gethsemane looking on the bowed back of Jesus. I hope that, as you read my reflections, they may give you something to consider.

I found it difficult to imagine sitting with the three disciples in Gethsemane at first, because I don't do much sitting in gardens at night. Occasionally I have a bedtime drink in the garden chair, and on very hot summer nights I have sometimes been tempted to sleep outside. Certainly, after the strain of a busy day, it would be easy to fall asleep unintentionally. It can be very pleasant in a garden when it's warm – very relaxing. If you had been to a special meal, a Passover meal which included wine, and all your circulation was busy digesting your food, it might be quite easy to fall asleep. If the garden was warm and quiet, it might be hard to keep your eyes open.

For the disciples, it was probably also something else. There are some deeper things at work here than simple tiredness after a good meal. We might call it "an avoidance mechanism". I first came across this in connection with a student whose family was in great distress, while she was very close to her final examinations. She was sleeping twenty hours out of every twenty-four – and not unnaturally was getting increasingly anxious about the fact that she was doing no revision at all. The stress was too much for her. The medical advice which she and I received then was that university final examinations can create more stress than soldiers experienced in the trenches in the First World War. Whether or not that is true, our bodies apparently have a mechanism to help us cope under extreme pressure. We simply "turn off", and sleep.

True, the disciples were probably tired, but they were also being called to sit and watch someone in extreme agony. It is difficult to stay beside people who are struggling. Perhaps you have watched someone in agony like that? Sometimes people speak of the privilege of sitting with people who are in that kind of situation, because they are very aware of the presence of God. But the person the disciples were watching was banging on heaven's door, and seemingly meeting with silence. Attention to a suffering other pierces your heart as well as theirs. It is exhausting. No wonder they went to sleep!

But the heart of this Gospel reading, which I find so profoundly disturbing and challenging, is that Jesus, who has been battering on heaven's door on his own account just a moment or two before, then turns to the disciples, finds them unequal to the task and asks them to watch not for him, but for themselves. He tells them to watch and pray for themselves! When that first struck me in the midst of a meditation, I found it very hard to believe that this was what he was really asking them to do. Was that what he was asking me to do too? I found that it was.

As I reviewed my prayer life, I realized that I was very busy doing all kinds of things as I responded to God. I was preoccupied with praying about situations and people, but was rarely praying that I might be kept in the time of trial. Of course it tripped off my tongue in the Lord's Prayer, "lead me not into temptation", but I had visions of cake shops or chocolate. Praying that I might be kept faithful through agonizing suffering as I resisted evil for the sake of the kingdom was out of the picture at that stage for me. I was praying for the work I do, praying for the preaching I was invited to do, praying for the people I teach, for the church's missions, for many different parts of the world, and for an endless list of individuals. But I did not pray very much for what was going on inside me, or for my faithfulness in times of trial. When I asked myself why this was, I found that there were three reasons:

1 I didn't think I needed to! When do I need God most? At that time it seemed as if I needed him when I stood to preach, or when I was tired. I needed him when I saw others struggling and could not help them myself. At that point I did not think I really needed him in any other kind of way. And yet, as I thought about it, I realized that gave the game away. "If I say I have no sin, I deceive myself" (see 1 John 1:8–9). If I think I have no weakness, then I have deceived myself, and the truth is not in

me. I need God's Holy Spirit inside me as well as outside. And I need him in the being as well as in the doing. I had to learn the painful lesson that I need him in myself, protecting me in troublesome times.

2 I didn't pray for myself, because I know the God to whom I pray: he does hear and he does answer. If I pray for myself, then he will hear and he will change things – and those "things" will be part of me, myself, and I'm not sure that I want that either! Watch and pray that you do not enter into temptation. It isn't every day that I am courageous enough to ask God to make me humble, kind, loving, strong in faith. I am not sure that I can cope with those gifts! Praying that I may not enter into temptation is about opening myself up, allowing him to change me and give me the gifts and graces of his Holy Spirit which will prepare me for suffering.

3 I did not want to learn to be vulnerable. Amazingly, Jesus in this extreme moment allows the disciples to see at least part of what is happening to him. To sit and watch his back bowed in prayer is to learn that the life I live in relation to God in Christ may need to be lived in an open place where other Christians can learn from me such little of the lessons I have learned from God through the Scriptures and the other means of grace, but most importantly through the lives of other Christians who have been willing to share themselves with me through fellowship or mentoring.

THE WOUNDS OF JESUS

Watching as we are bidden – so that we may love more

Standing, in my imagination, in the place where Jesus was flogged, or watching his slow and painful progress along the *via dolorosa*, cannot but increase my love for the one who endures all this for my sake.

> My song is love unknown,
> My Saviour's love for me,
> Love to the loveless shown,
> That they might lovely be.
> O, who am I,
> That for my sake
> My Lord should take
> Frail flesh and die?
> (Samuel Crossman, 1664)

Many of the passiontide hymns make clear that this has been the experience of countless Christians.

> When my love to God grows weak,
> When for deeper faith I seek,
> Then in faith, I turn to thee,
> Garden of Gethsemane.
> (John Reynell Wreford, 1837)

Many contemporary songs of renewal are love songs to Jesus, which some Christians, I know, find it hard to sing. Lent is a good time to watch Jesus in his suffering, until we can answer the question which he puts to us, as he put it to Peter: "Do you love me?" (John 21:15–17). If we find that the answer is "No", or "I don't know", then perhaps this Lent is a time to ask God to show us why we do not love Jesus, or why we are uncertain, and to begin the work of softening our heart by sending into it the Holy Spirit of love who enables us to love Jesus.

Watching as we are bidden – so that we may understand more

> Look how his bloodstained back
> in every part brings heaven before our eyes.

These words are sung in J.S. Bach's *St John's Passion*. Can this be true, or is this the extravagant language of music? What Bach does not mean is that heaven is in any way like this torn and beaten back. But in two short lines he has perceived what Christians have so often struggled to comprehend – that the love of God is seen in Jesus Christ's suffering for others, and that we are meant to gaze on this manifestation of the depth of God's concern for his suffering people, which leads him, in his incomparable compassion, to suffer with them.

> We may not know, we cannot tell,
> What pains he had to bear,
> But we believe it was for us
> He hung and suffered there.
>
> (Cecil Frances Alexander, 1848)

Pascal wrote that the heart has its reasons, which reason finds it hard to understand. Seeing and feeling are important ways of understanding what God has done for us in Jesus. They contribute a rich and vital embroidery to the tapestry of propositional theology which predominates in the epistles of the New Testament and in the writing of academic theology. We understand through our senses as well as through our minds. I think that is why St Paul says,

"I pray that the God of our Lord Jesus Christ, the Father of glory, may give you a spirit of wisdom and revelation as you come to know him, so that, *with the eyes of your heart enlightened*, you may know what is the hope to which he has called you. . ." (Ephesians 1:17–18, italics mine).

Lent could be a time when you sit and watch Jesus, asking God to enlighten the eyes of your heart, so that you may understand his purposes more fully.

Turning our back on the world

Ironically, it is not until we are able to turn our back on all that seems most attractive in the world that we can begin to see what it might be that God is calling us to do for him in the world. While we are committed to home ownership and mortgage repayment, for instance, we may not even consider offering our skills to a third-world country. Such a turning will always be a painful experience, since we come to love the world with all its rich variety as well as all its corruption. For very few Christians indeed will the call be to abandon the world completely, although that will come for some. For most, God will give us back some of what we have offered to him, as well as giving us other things besides. But an exploration of vocation, whether to engage with the world or to serve God in the Church, will inevitably pose us the question of whether we are willing to give up all for his sake. That is the question which we contemplate as we see Jesus turn his back on his previous life at baptism; as we see him turn his back on temptation and sin at Caesarea Philippi; as we see him give his back to the smiters in Jerusalem. Will I turn my back on good and evil? Will I allow my back to be smitten unrequited in the cause of the kingdom?

Gethsemane again!

Lord, why do you take me there . . . again . . . again . . .
again?
Is there no new place to see, no new word to hear, than
"watch and pray"
. . . again . . . again . . . again?
It's not the pain of watching you, though that is hard
enough,
Nor even the struggle against sleep, though that is lost,
. . . again . . . again . . . again . . .
But the demand to watch and pray (lest I fall into
temptation), which I find hard to take.
Why can't there be inoculation against evil?
Some miraculous transformation which removes the need
to watch and pray
. . . again . . . again . . . again?
The Lord says:
Because even in my suffering,
No, especially in my suffering,
You need to be with me,
to look to me, depend on me.
Your resistance to temptation depends on my resistance;
Your obedience to God's will depends on my obedience.
Your life depends on my death.
Your death depends on my life.
So watch and pray,
. . . again . . . again . . . again.
Watch me, look to me, wait on me and pray.
So that you may watch yourself,
look to yourself,
and wait until the answering comes to prayer.
For only so – in the watching –
is the grafting, life-bestowing bonding
which enables you-in-me and I-in-you
to enter not into temptation.

45

Conclusion

We cannot finally separate the wounds of Jesus from one another, just as we cannot finally separate the death of Jesus from his life and resurrection–ascension. So the fact that I have chosen here to focus on his back must not be read as if there were some things which could be said about this in a way which contradicts the rest of the passion narrative.

Nevertheless, we have seen that as disciples we need to keep Jesus in view, as we follow him in our day-to-day lives. There is also the sublime invitation to watch. We are invited to watch him struggling; to watch him being strengthened; to watch him resolving anew to walk to the trial and the cross; to watch him caring for us in the depths of his anguish; to watch him being flogged for us; to watch him hanging on the cross for us. In the midst of lives which are full of things to do, full of things to stop us thinking and facing deep questions, we are invited to watch, and to consider. That could be a deeply Lenten task.

Our watching will be enriched if we understand one of the recurrent themes which the New Testament employs as it seeks to probe the depths of God's purposes in Jesus Christ – the idea of substitution, of it being done for us, on our behalf. This idea is so deeply embedded in the New Testament that I do not think we can understand the gospel without grasping what it means. Jesus himself introduces the idea of substitution when he talks of his life as a ransom for many (Mark 10:45). It lies behind the sayings in John's Gospel that "The good shepherd lays down his life for the sheep" (10:11), and that "No one has greater love than this, to lay down one's life for one's friends" (15:13). It is one of the great motifs which Paul employs in a number of different contexts to elucidate the many implications of what has been achieved by the death and resurrection of Jesus: "For while we were still weak, at the right time Christ died for the ungodly. Indeed, rarely will anyone die for a righteous person – though perhaps for a good person someone might actually dare to die. But God proves his love for us in that while we were still sinners Christ died for us" (Romans 5:6–8).

We cannot consider this idea of substitution without reference to the covenant which spans Old and New Testaments as the way in which God's relationship to his people is to be understood. God's call throughout the Old Testament is for a people who will live in faithful covenant relationship with him. He promises to defend and protect his people and they are invited to live in dependence on him alone, by obeying his laws which are for their good. The history of the Old Testament, at one level, is a history of failed covenants: while God keeps his side of the agreement, the people do not. The New Testament records God's final covenant, which is radically different from what has been offered before (and is in that sense "new"), and in which God himself keeps both parts of the covenant. He continues to be faithful, but he also becomes human in Jesus of Nazareth, and so keeps the people's side of the agreement as well. This is why the New Testament says all that is now needed is for human beings to believe God has done all that is necessary and to accept it. This is the deepest substitution which God in Christ undertakes according to the gospel, and all the other substitutions flow out of this.

With this background it is possible to understand why the New Testament suggests two of the images we have cited above as ways of understanding what Jesus has done in allowing himself to be so brutally wounded. First, it is like a shepherd lying across the sheep pen opening and being the "living door" who will defend the sheep against any marauding animals. Rather than allow the defenceless sheep to die, the good shepherd suffers in their defence and if need be dies for them, "in their place". His death substitutes for theirs. Secondly, it is like someone who interposes himself into a situation where his friend is in mortal danger. History is littered with such examples. I read recently, for instance, that a young woman on a level crossing was able to push her boyfriend to safety out of the path of an oncoming train, but did not herself have time to flee, and so, tragically, was killed. Jesus is like someone who substitutes himself for his friends.

This is only one perspective on what is a complex set of texts which seek to explain why Jesus died. But it is important that we grasp this, if we are to have any appreciation of why our contemplation of the wounded back of Jesus might be an appropriate task for Lent. This is not a kind of voyeurism, nor is it wanton wallowing in suffering. It is a realistic attempt to understand the extent of Jesus' love for us as he has substituted himself and acted on our behalf. We will be looking at other aspects of this in the conclusions to subsequent chapters.

Questions and ideas

In a group

1 Ask one of the group to read the Gethsemane
narrative from one of the Gospels (Matthew 26:36–
46; Mark 14:32–42; Luke 22:39–46) slowly and
with good pauses, so that everyone can enter into
the story imaginatively. Allow a good space of time
at the end, before people are asked whether there is
anything that they want to share with the group.

2 Ask one of the group to read part of the passion
narrative from one of the Gospels (Matthew 27:24–
37; Mark 15:12–39) slowly and with good pauses,
so that everyone can enter into the story
imaginatively. Allow a good space of time at the
end, before people are asked whether there is
anything that they want to share with the group.

3 Pray the following litany together:

Merciful Lord, forgive us and restore us
For the way our society does not treat all human beings
with dignity.
Merciful Lord, forgive us and restore us
For neglect of the vulnerable and weak.
Merciful Lord, forgive us and restore us
For allowing financial security to become more important
than relationships.
Merciful Lord, forgive us and restore us
For all the places where dishonesty and deceit are taken
as normal.
Merciful Lord, forgive us and restore us
For allowing some schools to become places where
teachers are subject to harassment and assault.

Merciful Lord, forgive us and restore us
For giving young people so little hope that they turn to
*   drugs.*
Merciful Lord, forgive us and restore us
For Jesus' sake, Amen.

4 Write a litany which the group can use together, perhaps modelled on the one in (3) above, in which they take responsibility for confessing current social or ecclesiastical sins. It might be a good idea if each person contributes one part of such a litany.

5 Pray together for the victims of any corporate sins, which have been confessed as part of (4) above.

6 Consider what practical things this group could do to carry the burdens of those nearest to them in their area. Discuss what is holding you back from doing this, and consider whether you could begin something new together. Or could you join in with something worthwhile which others are already organizing?

7 Review what is actually being done by the local church community as a whole, to carry the burdens of others. While we can never do enough, is this a strong or weak area of church life? Consider what, if anything, you need to do about it.

By yourself

1 Read the Gethsemane narrative (Matthew 26:36–46; Mark 14:32–42; Luke 22:39–46) slowly and with pauses so that you have time to enter into the story. Where are you in the story? How do you feel? Is there anything which Jesus is asking you to do?

2 Read part of the passion narrative from one of the Gospels (Matthew 27:24–37; Mark 15:12–39) slowly and with good pauses, so that you have time to enter into the story imaginatively. Where are you in the story? How do you feel? Is there anything which the Lord has shown you afresh in this reading?

3 Give yourself a space of time (ten minutes, or perhaps more if you have plenty of time) to write down your answer to Jesus' question (or say it out loud if your speaking will not be overheard, and if you would find that easier): "Do you love me?"

4 Reflect on your own daily, weekly and monthly pattern of prayer. What space do you allow to pray that you yourself may not enter into temptation, and that you will be strengthened to face trials? How could you adjust your pattern if you need to?

5 Consider how far you have turned your back on the world in order to discover what God wants you to do in the world.

6 Let yourself explore what it feels like to know that Jesus endured this flogging for you.

A midday prayer for every day in Lent

Blessed Lord, at this hour you hung upon the cross for us and our redemption.
Stretch out your arms to us today, that we might know the forgiveness of all our sins.
For your name's sake, Amen.

FOR FURTHER READING

Raymond Brown, *The Death of the Messiah*, New York: Doubleday, 1994.

Martin Hengel, *Crucifixion*, London: SCM, 1977.

Gerard S. Loyan, *The Crucifixion of Jesus: History, Myth, Faith*, Minneapolis: Augsburg Fortress Press, 1995.

Russ Parker, *Healing Wounded History*, London: DLT, 2001.

HIS FEET
TEMPTATION AND CRUCIFIXION

His body

In the century in which Jesus lived, for most people, much of the time, their chief manner of travel was on foot. Although the Romans were famous for their roads, many local roads would have been of poor quality, so travel or transporting goods was hard work. Footwear varied considerably – from barefoot to boots. Roman soldiers had a closed boot with sole and upper, although the heat and the fact that they did not always fit exactly meant that these might not have been as comfortable as contemporary shoes can be. Many people wore sandals of various sorts – usually soles were "leather, wood or dried grass",[1] with loops attached and leather thongs passed through the loop to hold the sandal on the foot. Peasants had footwear with a semi-open top and a heavy sole, sometimes studded with nails, which protected their feet as they laboured in the fields. For everyday use completely closed footwear was too hot and therefore unusual. Indoors, slippers of coloured leather or fabric were worn.

The fact that people either went barefoot or used simple sandals had certain inevitable effects on their feet, which would have displayed all the calluses and wear which are the consequence of that way of life. As an invited member of the Lambeth Conference for Anglican bishops in 1998, I was part of the mutual foot-washing ceremony that took place there. I had never before come so close to so many feet which almost certainly looked much the same as the feet of ordinary people in the time of Jesus. It was a privilege to be able to wash the feet of one of my fellow conference members. I discovered that my Western feet were much more pampered than the feet of those from overseas, Africa especially. In long winters and short summers, wearing sandals or going barefoot is rare for me, and my shoes protect my feet from the wear and tear caused by walking on dirt roads. But Jesus, I guessed, would have had just such hardened feet.

Since people in Jesus' day walked either barefoot or in sandals, their feet were not protected from the dirt as they progressed along roads which were essentially rough tracks, where rubbish fell unhindered. These roads were also travelled by animals, whose recent presence was always visible from the droppings which they left. In towns, where there was no rubbish collection, people swept out their homes into the street. Not only dust but any household rubbish might be cleared out, so it would be hard to prevent your feet becoming very dirty as you walked around. Over the years, we know that people eventually had to step down into their homes, as streets and alleys receiving regular sweepings gradually grew higher than the floor-level of the houses. Hygiene was probably poor, and infection could be picked up through dirt on the feet. There were few sewage systems, although there were rules about where and how people were to discharge their bowels and bladders (see Deuteronomy 23:13–14).

Work which has been done in recent years to explore the ways of life of the people of Jesus' time highlights the low rainfall in the region and the lack of water necessary for maintaining personal cleanliness. Complete washing was probably infrequent unless people lived near running water, or were willing to go to Roman baths, which many Jews refused to do. There is, however, evidence that feet would be washed regularly, as well as hands and faces.

There are some biblical references which suggest that washing a person's feet was part of the hospitality which people in this part of the world would offer their guests. Abraham said to his three visitors, "Let a little water be brought, and wash your feet, and rest yourselves. . ." (Genesis 18:4), and it was certainly expected at the meal which Jesus planned for his disciples, although they were reluctant to perform this menial task (John 13). Some of the purification rituals which priests were tasked to perform included foot-washing (Exodus 30:18–19), and it seems that there were special vessels in which this was done (Psalm 60:8; 108:9).

Jesus' feet

Jesus' feet took him into many different parts of Palestine, and into countless situations where the power of God was needed – to the family home of Jairus, whose daughter needed healing and new life (Mark 5:23); into the boat so that he could talk to the crowds (Luke 5:1–3); across the fields where grain was growing (Mark 2:23–28). They carried him to Jerusalem when he knew that the destiny which awaited him there was to suffer and die (Luke 19:28). He climbed mountains (Matthew 5:1), walked on water (Mark 6:48), and swept into the temple where his firm stand against corruption challenged the racketeering which benefited the elite at the expense of the peasants and precluded prayer to God (Mark 11:15–19). His feet, almost certainly, resembled the feet of those around me at the Lambeth Conference, roughened by much tough walking.

There is some ambiguity as to whether Jesus prohibited the wearing of sandals on the missionary journey for which he commissioned the Twelve in Matthew 10:10, or whether the meaning is that they were not to take a spare pair of sandals. If they were not to wear sandals at all, they would be regarded by those to whom they went as especially poor (Luke 15:22). Alternatively, it might have been intended to demonstrate that they were engaged on a sacred task, since there was a ban on wearing sandals on the temple mount because of its holiness. The command to go without sandals is thus very radical, as is the prohibition on carrying a bag. Another reason that has been suggested is the need for utter dependence on God and his provisions. So the disciples might have been barefoot to demonstrate their poverty, the holiness of their task, or their utter dependence on God. If they did indeed go barefoot, for whatever reason, then we must wonder whether Jesus himself wore sandals. Such a radical demand by Jesus (which the other Gospels do not record – Luke 10:4 has "carry no sandals" and means an extra pair; Mark 6:8–9 says they are "to take nothing . . . but to wear sandals . . .") could surely not have been made unless it was his custom already.

Whatever footwear (if any) Jesus wore, like every other itinerant he would need to wash his feet or have them washed when he was invited for a meal – particularly since at special meals people ate reclining with their feet adjacent to other guests. As guests reclined, their sandals were removed from their feet. This is the background to the story in Luke 7:36–50, where Jesus points out that his host has neglected to provide water for his feet (verse 44). Jesus was trying to help his host see why he was prepared to allow a sinful woman to touch him, when she wept over his feet and wiped them with her hair, kissing them and anointing them with expensive ointment. Simon the Pharisee was scandalized that such actions should be allowed by someone he had thought of as a prophet, but whose prophetic powers he was now coming to conclude were false, since Jesus obviously did not recognize the sinful nature of the woman who was acting in this intimate way, in a semi-public place. Jesus, however, accepted the woman's actions as a sign that her sins had been forgiven and acknowledged what she did as the outward sign of her service and devotion to the one whose life and preaching had made possible for her a renewed relationship with God. Jesus, the true prophet, not only knew the nature of the woman, but he also knew her recent history: she used to be a sinner, but now that her sins had been forgiven, her love was overflowing from a grateful heart.

Touched by the dirt of the world and already honoured by the tears of the grateful penitent, these feet were ready, when the time came, to walk to Calvary for their piercing.

His wounds

Nailed to the cross

The Gospels give us very little evidence of the exact way in which Jesus was fixed to the cross. Christians have assumed that it was by nails through his feet because, in the narrative of the risen Jesus appearing to Thomas and the other disciples, Jesus mentions the mark of the nails in his hands, and it is logical to suppose that his feet were also nailed (John 20:27). This is also implied by the words of Jesus to the disciples walking to Emmaus: "Look at my hands

and my feet; see that it is I myself. Touch me and see. . ."
(Luke 24:39). As I explained earlier, however, sometimes
people were lashed to the cross, so although it may well be
the case that Jesus' feet were nailed, we need to recognize
that we cannot be absolutely certain of this.

There is plenty of evidence that not all those who were
crucified had their feet fixed to the cross in the same way.
There are a number of contemporary documents which
allude to this, but in 1968 an archaeological discovery was
made which has considerably increased our understanding.
This discovery brought to light the only known example of
the remains of a crucified person.[2] His bones were found
north-east of Jerusalem in an ossuary, a box made for bones,
which has his name – Yehochanan – inscribed on it. When
his executioners or family took his body from the cross,
they were unable to remove the four-and-a-half-inch nail
from his right heel bone, and so when his bones were discovered there was still a nail in them: "A small wooden
board had been nailed to the outside of his heel to prevent
him from tearing his leg off the nail's small head."[3] In nailing the man to the cross, this nail had been bent. It could
not therefore be removed through the man's body after his
death, so they had cut the upright post away. What remains
today is the heel bone, the nail, the small wooden board
and a piece of olive wood from the upright stake of the
cross. His legs had not been broken, as was sometimes the
custom. He was probably in his twenties and executed in
the first century. This is an important piece of evidence
which helps us to understand how some people were nailed
to the cross. It shows that holding the weight of a person on
a cross was possible because the nailing was through the
bones – a desperately painful process. Scholars think it
likely that this man had been lashed to the crossbeam, since

there are no nail marks in the hands or arm bones, but that his heels had been nailed on either side of the upright stake of the cross using two nails, supplemented by the small wooden planks.

We do not have to conclude that this was the same method used in the case of Jesus – we simply do not know. We have no reliable evidence as to whether there were four nails used in his crucifixion, one for each hand and foot, or whether there were only three, one nail going through both feet with one foot folded over the other. Artistic portrayals of the crucifixion often show the latter method. Despite the fact that the nailing would have been excruciatingly painful, there is no comment on the pain of Jesus in the Gospels.

Sometimes, when the feet were nailed over one another, there was a footrest at the base of the cross, which enabled the crucified person to raise his body and take the weight off his arms in order to breathe more freely. We have no evidence that such a rest was present in the crucifixion of Jesus, and the fact that his death came unexpectedly swiftly (Mark 15:44) suggests that it was not there.

Those who took Jesus down from the cross would need to remove the nails from the cross in order to free him, and would want, if it were possible, to remove them also from the body as an act of respect. We must assume that this happened. You will see this depicted in some religious art.

Freedom and power

As we consider this image of the suffering Saviour, fixed to the cross, we face the intense contrast between who we believe him to be and what we see happening to him. Theologians often talk about these and other similar contrasts as "dialectics", since neither side of the paradox can be resolved into the other. I think that we can consider this through two themes: the freedom of the one who is fixed with extraordinary finality to the cross, and the power of the powerless one.

Everything God has shown us about himself suggests that his freedom is infinite and that he always chooses to act in ways which are consistent with his character, but that his freedom is far beyond anything we can comprehend or experience. Nothing, and no one, can say to God, "You must." There are no "oughts" for God, no standard by which he must act, only standards by which he freely chooses to act because it pleases him to be self-consistent. This freedom we know is shared by Father, Son and Holy Spirit, in their life of mutual love and indwelling.

This freedom is shaped by God's decision to create the universe and to "make space" for it to exist in utter dependence on him, but also to grant it a degree of independence. That first "shaping" is echoed in the decision of God for his Son to become incarnate in the world as the truly human person Jesus. I have deliberately used the word "shaped" because I do not think we can automatically presuppose that either creation or incarnation limits God's freedom. In one way, creation and incarnation open up possibilities to God which did not exist before he freely chose to engage in them. But, in electing creation and incarnation, God freely chooses both the new possibilities and what we see as their limitations. God freely chooses to be bound by his own norms of creation as he relates to it in its time. God freely chooses to be bound by his own norms of being human as he experiences being human in time. But as he does both of these things, he does not abandon his own sovereignty in, over and through these circumstances.

If I may use a very down-to-earth illustration, it is like a person holding an egg in his hand and understanding extremely well the exact strengths and fragilities of eggshells. Such a person can do things with an egg without fracturing it and smashing it to bits. Such a person works within a framework of possibilities with eggs which may be far greater than any cook, casually breaking eggs to make an omelette, has ever contemplated. That seems to be like the situation which we see in the relationship of God to the creation and his being made flesh in incarnation. Our presuppositions about how God might relate to the world depend on our limited understanding both of the world and of God. The same is true about incarnation.

What we see in incarnation is God expressing his sovereign freedom in choosing to be limited to this time, this man, this place – though never in a way which is as limited as we might think it would have to be to maintain his true humanity. We discover in him, for instance, that one can be truly human without sinning. We discover in him that one can be truly human without accepting as inevitable the sickness of others. We discover in him that one can be truly human without accepting the rule of anyone other than God himself. Only God knows what it would have taken to "fracture" the humanity of the Son of God by imposing on it more of the divine freedom than it could endure. We cannot see that, because God chose not to fracture his humanity.

What we can see, and what we struggle to understand, is the interplay between the created order and God incarnate in the "framework of possibilities" in which God has chosen to work in Jesus Christ. But we also see unexpected things about the nature of God: that he can freely choose to be finally limited in space and time to the suffering of the cross, and that he can and does give himself willingly to that fixing which locates him in this place of powerless suffering. His feet are nailed, without him giving up his freedom and his power to do and be otherwise. We glimpse this occasionally in the New Testament, for instance in the dialogue between Pilate and Jesus in John's Gospel, or in Paul's discussion in 1 Corinthians of the power of God in folly and wisdom.

We can perhaps best understand this tension between power and powerlessness as a series of parts in an expanding telescope. In this particular telescope there are six tubes which can be fully extended, but we only see them one at a time, as we travel from the thickest to the thinnest "tube". If we think of the widest part of the telescope as all that can be seen protruding out of a window, then we will only see part of the telescope, until the person using it pushes more and more of it into the open air. The widest tube is part of it, but there are five more parts to be explored. I shall explain each part below, in terms of which character in the narrative has power, and which character is powerless.

1 As Jesus stands in the presence of Pilate before he is finally condemned to death, Pilate says, "Do you refuse to speak to me? Do you not know that I have power to release you, and power to crucify you?" (John 19:10). From Pilate's perspective, he has power and Jesus is powerless. There is, of course, truth in this. Jesus has already been flogged and there is no way that this weakened person can escape the might of Rome. But this is only one of six possible perspectives.

2 Jesus is only in this "powerless" position because he took certain decisions earlier in his life. I think that

is what John 10:18 refers to, at least in part: "No one takes it [my life] from me, but I lay it down of my own accord. I have power to lay it down. . ." Jesus is like a contemporary protester against some social evil. It is true that once such people have broken the law and been arrested for trespass, the police have the power to put them in a cell, or the judge has the power to imprison them when found guilty, but that is only the case because they decided not to go swimming but to go protesting instead, knowing the consequences full well. In this scenario, Jesus has the power, and Pilate only has immediate power to execute him because Jesus has made the decision to preach, to go to Jerusalem, to challenge authority in the temple and to imply by his actions and teaching that he has a special relationship with God. So there is a sense in which Jesus has power and Pilate is "powerlessly" – we might say routinely – responding to events beyond his control.

3 As we continue to "travel up the telescope" we see that in the next "tube" there is a different arrangement of power. Here Pilate has power, because of the delegated authority given to rulers by God himself. "Jesus answered him [Pilate], 'You would have no power over me unless it had been given you from above. . .'" (John 19:11). In this perspective, Pilate has legitimate power to execute, and Jesus as a private individual is subject to the rule of Rome, and as such is powerless.

4 From this stage in our journey along the telescope we look at this narrative from the perspective of the

prologue to John's Gospel. That requires us to see Jesus not only as a human person, but as the Word of God incarnate (1:14). From this viewpoint, the power and powerlessness counters change once more. Now, we need to recognize that God (Father, Son and Holy Spirit) is powerful enough to choose freely and lovingly that the Son (or Word) of God should become human and be capable of dying and rising again. So we can make sense of John 10:18 in full: "No one takes it [my life] from me, but I lay it down of my own accord. I have power to lay it down, *and I have power to take it up again. I have received this command from my Father*" (italics mine). In this way of viewing things, Pilate is powerless, playing a bit part in a cosmic drama which he can only dimly perceive. Jesus (with the Father and the Holy Spirit) is powerful, and is exercising power even through apparent powerlessness.

5 We need to recognize, however, that there is another way of seeing this scene. The divine decision to become human so as to suffer and die is a decision to give away power in order that eternal life may be available to all people: "For God so loved the world that he gave his only Son, so that everyone who believes in him may not perish but may have eternal life" (John 3:16). Looked at from this standpoint, Pilate has power because God, the Son of God, has decided to exercise his power by giving away power – the power of self-preservation. The Son of God has given away his power and become powerless. Having given away his inviolability, his feet can be pierced.

6 The final point of view reaches back into our exploration of God's freedom, for it emphasizes that God is sovereign and free to decide how to be. Hence God, the Son of God, has power (which he is free to use in any way that is consistent with his Godliness) to lay down his life and take it up again. Thus Pilate has no power in himself faced with the Son of God. The unfolding Johannine narrative makes that very clear. It is undoubtedly the decision of Pilate to order crucifixion, but the way the dialogue unfolds in John 18:28–19:16 portrays Pilate as a weak and ineffectual ruler struggling with events too big for him to control. In the words of 1 Corinthians, the folly and weakness of the cross is shown to be the power and wisdom of God at work in the world for those who will believe (1:18).

With so many levels of interpretation, and so many ways of reading the interchanges of "powerful" and "powerless", perhaps it is understandable that Pilate comes across as if he feels things are whizzing out his control. When we look at Jesus, by contrast, we see his freedom freely offered up as he is fixed to the cross, and his power dedicated to saving the powerless – through his own powerlessness.

His life – temptation and crucifixion

In what ways were the feet of Jesus prepared for crucifixion? Undoubtedly Jesus knew the first Psalm, which pronounces happy the person who does ". . . not follow the advice of the wicked, or take the path that sinners tread" (verse 1). In this section we will explore the way in which Jesus' feet went towards the will of God throughout his life, so that they were accustomed to walking towards godliness and away from evil. The places in the Gospels which make this most plain are the places where we are shown the temptations to walk otherwise which Jesus endured.[4]

A test of faithfulness

The Synoptic Gospels narrate in their different ways the classic beginning of the temptations which coincided with the baptism and wilderness period (Matthew 4:1–11; Mark 1:12–13; Luke 4:1–13), but which continue throughout his ministry – I believe until the very last scenes on the cross, a point I shall discuss further below. At every point, it is as if Satan is probing the resolution of Jesus to fulfil his God-given commission, exploring whether he will cut corners or walk away from God's call. All the temptations were a trial of Jesus' faithfulness to God. We might say that they were also trials of whether Jesus could hold fast to who he really was.

Jesus had just been confirmed in his commission to be God's Son and had been filled with the Holy Spirit, when the Spirit drove him into the wilderness. That testing time was like a limbering-up exercise – preparing Jesus for what was to come. In the Old Testament Satan was connected to two things: trying the pious, and standing in opposition to the elect of God, frustrating God's purposes and destroying the relationship between God and God's elect. We can see both those things happening once again in the various narratives at the beginning of Jesus' ministry.[5]

Three titles are used for Jesus by the early Christians and by classic writers on theology. We hail him as prophet, priest and king: prophet because he is Spirit-anointed and speaks the words of God to us; priest because he offers the one perfect sacrifice of himself on the cross; king because,

as Messiah, he brings in God's kingdom and will reign for
ever. I think that we might see the temptations as assaults
on Jesus' call to be prophet, priest and king. Using Luke's
narrative (4:1–13), the temptation to change stones into
bread might be read as a temptation for Jesus to use his
God-given power to feed himself when his call is to feed
others, and that not chiefly with material relief but with
himself, the bread of heaven. This is a challenge to use
God's power to maintain himself rather than to give himself freely for others; it is a challenge to his priestly self-
sacrifice. The temptation to rule the world by worshipping
Satan is certainly a challenge to his kingly role; this role will
be (and already is) his by God-given delegated power and
it is not to be achieved by aiming for glory (verse 6). The
temptation to cast himself off the pinnacle of the temple is
a challenge to his prophetic role: later the people ask for
signs because they believe that is what prophets can deliver
(Mark 8:11). Jesus refuses this both now and later on.[6]

All the other occasions in the Gospels when Jesus is
tested could be said to display similar characteristics. Each
is an attempt to upset or overturn his call – as priest to offer
himself as the supreme self-sacrifice; as prophet to make
God's perspective known without buying into the contemporary view of God's priorities; as king to rule in humility and suffering. Only one example of each can be given
here.

When Peter remonstrates with Jesus for suggesting that
the way ahead of him will involve suffering, rejection and
execution, before resurrection, we might consider that this
is an attempt to lead him away from his priestly call to offer
himself (Mark 8:31–33).

When Jesus is challenged to declare whether or not it is
right to pay taxes to Caesar (Matthew 22:15–22), the nature

of his rule over people is being probed. Will he side with Rome and authenticate their use of force, or will he rebel against Rome by declaring that their rule has no authority over God's people? In either case, will he claim, by answering the question directly, that he has authority to decide these matters? The enigmatic tossing back of the matter to the questioners allows him to escape the corner into which they thought they had backed him, without prejudice to his real identity as the suffering servant king.

When people ask him for a sign from heaven (Matthew 16:1–4), they are testing his understanding of what it means to be the prophet of God. Jesus refuses their request on the grounds that there are already enough signs, could they, or would they, but read them. His clear implication is that he can both identify and read these signs, but since the people are ignoring what God is already revealing to them, he is not at their disposal to call up incontrovertible signs which will convince them one way or another.

Of course, there is only one Jesus, and he has only one call, so there is a real sense in which his identity and commission are far more intertwined than this discussion has so far indicated. In the end, his call to be prophet, priest and king could be regarded as the three legs of a stool on which he is invited to sit. Cut off any one of these three, and the vocation (like the stool) is destroyed.

Throughout his ministry, therefore, we might say that Jesus is willing to walk the way of the cross, even though he is being tempted not to do so. We know he thought of it in that way, for he said, "You are those who have stood by me in my trials" (Luke 22:28). His fortitude grows day by day, so that he will be ready to endure even the final testings of his intention in the last hours of his life.

The final test

While it is true that the devil departs from Jesus for a time (Luke 4:13), he returns on various occasions to tempt him not to fulfil his mission. Satan's final appearance comes at the very end of Jesus' life, during the trials and on the cross. Satan had one last attempt to overturn God's purposes, and each of Jesus' roles – prophet, priest and king – are challenged in the last hours of his life.

As Jesus is slapped in the face, he is challenged, even though he is blindfolded, to prophesy who has done it. Jesus was generally regarded as a prophet, but there were two prophecies around which the accusations against him centred. One was the reported claim that if the temple was destroyed, Jesus had said that he would rebuild a temple, not made with hands, in three days (Mark 14:58). The second claim was one he made directly in their hearing: that the Son of Man would be "seated at the right hand of the Power, and coming with the clouds of heaven" (Mark 14:62). Perhaps because of his general reputation, or because of the specific contents of the trial, there begins a process of mocking. Maybe they hope to show that he cannot "prophesy" or guess right on even simple things. Or, perhaps more sinisterly, they are intent on preventing him ever trying again. It has been pointed out that even while Jesus refused to use his God-given gift in this way, he remained a true prophet, because his own prophecies of his forthcoming suffering and death given earlier in the Gospels were being fulfilled (e.g., Mark 8:31), and he was also fulfilling the Old Testament prophecies about him (found, for instance, in Isaiah 53).[7] There is a sense in which only his refusal to respond to their immediate calls for evidence of his prophetic gifts would enable him to demonstrate once and for all that he was the true prophet of God, whose prophetic gifts exceeded their comprehension.

After the flogging and the sentence of death, Jesus' kingship is mocked as he is dressed in purple and crowned with thorns, and acclaimed as king (Mark 15:16–20). He remains silent throughout this ordeal – refusing to doubt or deny his true messiahship in order to escape the suffering.

While he hangs on the cross, he is taunted by the passers-by, the religious leaders, and by those crucified with him. He is faced with the temptation to leave the cross, and thereby abandon his vocation as the true high priest offering himself for others (Mark 15:29–32). He resists that temptation even in the throes of his failing physical strength. By now he is close to death, and so he remains true to the call of God upon his life.

These three temptations at the end of Jesus' life are all probing his true vocation. The third, which in one sense is the most crucial, is of triple intensity. First the passers-by deride him, then the chief priests and scribes, and finally those who are crucified with him. Although they appeal again to the prophetic and kingly titles of Jesus (respectively, "Aha! You who would destroy the temple and build it in three days. . ." [Mark 15:29], and, "Let the Messiah, the King of Israel, come down. . ." [Mark 15:32]), both of these taunts and the final one are all aimed at tempting him to exercise the kind of power which he had rejected in the first recorded temptations, to misuse God's power for his own selfish purposes. There the proposal was, "If you are the Son of God, throw yourself down from here. . ." (Luke 4:9), whereas now the proposal is, "If you are the King of the Jews, save yourself!" (Luke 23:37). The taunts are all directed at the priestly self-offering of himself as sacrifice for the sins of the whole world. They fail. His love keeps him on the cross; his feet were made for nailing. And iron-ically, the fact that he remains fixed there, and does not come down from the cross, shows that he is truly prophet, priest and king. This alone will call forth the first confes-sion of faith in the crucified: "Truly this man was God's Son!" (Mark 15:39).

It was because of Jesus' determination to walk into the desert, to walk in the way of his calling, and to walk into Jerusalem, that it was possible for his feet to be nailed to the cross. His feet had been pointing in the direction of our salvation throughout his life. It is precisely this willingness to go to each of these places which makes the fulfilment of Isaiah's prophecy possible: "How beautiful upon the moun-tains are the feet of the messenger . . . who brings good news" (Isaiah 52:7). It is because Jesus is willing to go to the places of struggle and suffering that he is the bringer of good news. Contemplating his nailed feet, we exclaim, "How beautiful!"

What does this mean for us as a faith community?

Walking the way of the cross together

There are two clear ways in which our consideration of the nailed feet of Jesus might influence our Christian life. The first is the invitation to walk together in the footsteps of Jesus, as he goes to the cross. Peter puts it like this to the converted slaves whom he is addressing, but also to all who will read his letter: "For to this you have been called, because Christ also suffered for you, leaving you an example, so that you should follow in his steps" (1 Peter 2:21). In this part of Peter's letter he was applying the Christian faith to two groups of people who would find it hardest to balance the freedom that was now theirs in the gospel with their being bound in social relationships which did not admit of very much freedom. Those two groups were slaves and wives. They would find this tension especially hard when they were bound to owners and husbands who were not yet converted to Jesus. This is exactly the tension which we explored earlier in the case of God becoming human in the person of Jesus, truly free, yet truly bound. For them also, there would be the experience of the Holy Spirit's empowering to live the Christian life, which must be lived out in the daily disempowerment of their social setting.

In the words "to this you have been called", Peter is referring to their vocation to do good even when they are suffering unjustly, trusting in God throughout. The example which Jesus has given us is like a written sampler which guides a child who is learning to write. So when Christians encounter trials or suffering, we know how to endure them: as Jesus did, without retaliation and with continued trust in God.

None of this is easy, which is why I have taken the hint from this passage that addresses people together, not one by one. If we are to endure the times of trial, and if we are to walk in Jesus' footsteps, we will need the encouragement of one another and the support of fellow Christians. In every period of history, Christians have recognized this and have used many different structures to ensure that such needs are met. Today cell groups, house groups, spiritual mentoring or soul friends are all ways of enabling us to give each other mutual support. Any of these arrangements also involves us in the tensions of being free yet bound; of having power yet experiencing powerlessness.

Human beings value their freedom highly and find it hard to be mutually accountable. One of the continued temptations will be to walk in our own way and to express our God-given freedom to do and think as we like. But we are invited to recognize that we belong together and that there is still the call of Jesus on our life to give up our freedoms and to follow in the way to which he calls us. The fact that Christians have often found that his service is "perfect freedom" does not mean that this is how it will look at the beginning of any part of the journey. Equally, we may want to continue our delusion that we are powerful enough to make this journey alone. In the West we live in cultures which seem to suggest to us that the aim of adult human living is independence. Such a view is sold to us in the media through many advertisements. The opposite is often portrayed as a regrettable dependence, which we are forced to accept in infancy and extreme old age. Many fight to postpone the day when that is necessary. Christian living, however, is about dignified dependence. We do need one another, but we do not demean those who need our assistance – and we need to be delivered from the fear that we will be treated like children or those with advanced senility if we admit to one another that we find it hard to walk in Jesus' footsteps and that we need the help of those around us.

So many Christians cut themselves off from the helpful fellowship which God intends for us, rather than admit to those around them the powerlessness which they feel when they are struggling. I have so often observed that Satan loves to "divide and conquer". Seeing that this is the case, perhaps we need to think again how much we share one another's burdens in this area. At the very least, we need to

ask for one another's prayers, which will be more significant than we can ever guess.

I do not advise what I have not found to be essential
myself. I am fortunate in being able to talk regularly to a
spiritual director, who asks the hard questions about how I
am following in Jesus' footsteps, and who encourages me.
Another person whose vocation to pray keeps her in one
community, and whose physical incapacity keeps her chiefly
in bed, ministers to me by her supportive prayer. People
often ask me how I manage to do so much, and I know that
the answer lies largely in this person's prayer ministry. What
I am enabled to do is all on the back of the ministry of other
Christians whose lives and prayers support me. I know that
I am too weak to follow Jesus alone; I need the companions
he has provided for me along the way.

Washing one another's feet

The question of how we engage in this mutual support
brings us to the second way in which our contemplation of
Jesus' nailed feet might influence our Christian life. It is pic-
tured for us in the story of Jesus washing his disciples' feet
(John 13:1–17).[8] I wonder whether Jesus was inspired to do
this by the humility of the woman who, out of sheer love
for him, washed his feet with her tears. We cannot know the
answer to that now, but clearly Jesus' love for his disciples,
even when they are at their most resistant to walking in his
serving footsteps, overflows in the actions of stripping, gird-
ing, washing and wiping. Some writers point out that social
convention was very strong at that time, so part of the reason why Peter was horrified was because Jesus, their teacher
and leader, was taking the part of a slave.[9]

Jesus' teaching, however, is extremely clear: "So if I, your
Lord and Teacher, have washed your feet, you also ought

to wash one another's feet" (John 13:14). Many Christians have preferred not to take this command seriously and have never washed the feet of another disciple. Even those who are committed to obeying other commands such as baptizing and breaking bread together often ignore this plain command. As an act of service it cannot mean exactly the same for those whose feet are normally well covered by socks and shoes, but we do well to consider why we never obey the command even in a ceremonial way. That alone, of course, is not enough. We need to serve one another in ways which are as practical and perhaps as socially uninviting as the service of foot-washing was for the first disciples.

But why is it important also to do exactly the thing which Jesus has bidden us to do? One of the consequences of this act of obedience is to break down the barriers which so often exist between Christians. Washing someone else's feet is a very intimate and personal act – even in a public place. We urgently need to see how important this is. Formal Christianity has often sanitized the gospel so that it is no longer possible to see why the people of Jesus' time were offended by what he taught. Equally, we have learned the gospel as if we could remain strangers from one another and still follow in Jesus' footsteps. We cannot.

By a number of strategies, Jesus moves his disparate disciples from being strangers to one another, to being companions on the way of the cross, and to being "family", where mutual love and support are always appropriate. At the time of Jesus, descent and family lineage were immensely important – hence the provision of the family trees in both Matthew and Luke, and the rather more radical lineage offered in the prologue of John who, like Luke, names Jesus as "Son of God". In the time of Jesus, the family into which you were born placed you in society, much as it still does today in many parts of the world. The Gospels show how Jesus began to break down the traditional family ties and proposed that those who were his followers would be counted as his family, indeed that they would have a new family lineage to make them sons and daughters of God.

This theme is picked up in Paul's writings, which make much of the idea that we are adopted children: ". . . when the fullness of time had come, God sent his Son, born of a woman, born under the law, in order to redeem those who were under the law, so that we might receive adoption as children. And because you are children, God has sent the Spirit of his Son into our hearts, crying, 'Abba! Father!' So you are no longer a slave but a child, and if a child then also an heir, through God" (Galatians 4:4–7). We may say that the first step of walking together in the way of the cross is being adopted into God's family. This is not something which is earned. It has been given to us. We do not choose our biological or Christian brothers and sisters, but we are invited to love one another, and to wash one another's feet as a way of learning what it might mean to serve one another, and to relate to one another with dignified dependence.

Becoming a disciple of Jesus transforms relationships, because it brings into relationship people who had no relationship previously and who are now offered the chance to relate as family. When the Church is functioning at its best, this is the reason why it attracts many dysfunctional people, because in it they find the accepting love and support which society as a whole does not readily offer them. And when it most clearly manifests the signs of the coming kingdom, the Church loves, honours and receives such people's service in whatever form they can offer it.

What does this mean for us personally?

Resisting temptation

We will consider two kinds of temptation in this section. The first is the kind which Jesus is portrayed as encountering throughout his life, the trials which try to subvert his mission. The second is the kind which we more often envisage when we consider this subject, temptations to lie, or steal, or cheat. We need to recognize immediately that temptation will be with us throughout our lives, so that we can develop God's ways of confronting and overcoming it. Not *recognizing* temptation – not temptation itself – is the more worrying sign in the Christian life.

All the temptation which Jesus encountered was focused on his unique identity and mission, so in one way his experience will be far removed from that of any ordinary Christian life. But since God has given us all an identity and mission or vocation which is truly our own, we can expect that it will come under trial and temptation in many different ways. What might this mean for an individual?

One way of thinking about this is to use the idea of the "armour of God" which St Paul describes in Ephesians 6:10–18. He speaks of the belt of truth, the breastplate of righteousness, the shoes of readiness to proclaim the gospel of peace, the shield of faith, the helmet of salvation and the sword of the Spirit. All of these, Paul emphasizes, are available to us as Christians. My supposition is that if these are the provisions for defence, they may give us an indication of what we might encounter. A person who has come to repentance and belief in Jesus Christ has been given a new and right relationship with God. The breastplate of righteousness assures our heart that this is indeed the case, and enables us to keep a right relationship with God and with

THE WOUNDS OF JESUS

others as the very heart of the gospel. We may be tempted to believe that God has not really adopted us, or to think that somehow we are not worthy of such a relationship. Indeed, we are not worthy. Yet God in his grace has adopted us, and all attempts to make us think otherwise will inevitably undermine our capacity to live out the truth of our new identity, which is the basis for all the ethical exhortations in Paul's letters. For instance, he suggests that "if you have been raised with Christ" – and Paul is sure Christians have been (Colossians 3:1), then you should "put to death . . . whatever in you is earthly" (Colossians 3:5) and "clothe yourselves with compassion, kindness, humility, meekness and patience" (Colossians 3:12). Thus the right relationship with God is the truth about ourselves which we need to keep tightly fixed upon us, using the belt of truth provided. This will remind us that we need to be living the truth as well as speaking the truth.

If we are indeed the adopted children of God – and this is the relationship which God is offering to all those who repent and believe in Jesus – then we need to have on our feet the shoes of readiness to proclaim to all and sundry this gospel of peace with God. But of course, that readiness or certainty of what the gospel is will be under continual attack. The opposition would prefer that we have neither the confidence nor the courage to speak about Jesus, who has trodden the way to the cross and allowed his feet to be nailed there in order that everyone may be brought into this right relationship with God. But the shoes of readiness are ours – we only need to claim them from the God who provides them. God knows that many of our temptations will come through our minds, which is why he has provided the helmet of salvation to protect us from all the suggestions which assault us from outside, or which we dream up inside. Trusting in God, taking up the shield of faith, is the best antidote to everything that tries to make us see things from any perspective other than the perspective of God himself.

Finally, we have one offensive weapon with which to resist the trials that will come. This is the sword of the Spirit, which is the Word of God. If individual Christians are weak and unable to resist the trials that come their way, then it may be because they have neglected the Word of God, which the Holy Spirit makes a lively Word to us when we read and ponder it. There are three ways in which we may think of this.

First, when we are saturated in something, we automatically soak it up – whether it is television, or the Bible. When I was studying in the 1970s, I needed to learn German. A family was kind enough to invite me to stay with them for a month. I was forbidden to speak or read English. I even had to play Scrabble in German. Gradually I absorbed enough of the language to conduct a conversation. Eventually, to my horror, I found myself praying in German one day! (It wasn't that I minded learning German – it was just that I thought I could keep it on the "outside", but then I discovered that it had penetrated this most intimate part of my life.) Taking up the sword of the Spirit, which is the word of God, is like being saturated in another language and culture. It becomes second nature, and eventually it needs to become *first* nature, just as an adopted language does for people who live for decades in another country and have little or no contact with home. It is not a matter of being able to quote Scripture, it is a matter of our whole life being shaped by God and God's purposes. This only happens through a lifetime of prayer and study of God's word.

If this is a whole new world for you, then do not be frightened of what may be involved. There are many different ways in which you can begin this lifetime habit. Any Christian bookshop will be able to let you have Bible reading notes, or a minister would be glad to help you get started. Becoming saturated involves swimming in all of Scripture.

Secondly, we need to notice that there are some parts of the Bible where God seems to speak to us most directly. It is like swimming in the sea, and finding that there are some warm or tranquil spots where the going is easier. These are places to relish and return to, since they may enable us to get stronger in our swimming and move out into colder or more turbulent waters. So if a particular psalm seems to speak to your circumstances, it is fine to read it every day for a week or a month. Better still, learn it off by heart so that you can pray it wherever you are. Do not let it be the only passage of Scripture which you read, however. As with the food we eat, a varied diet is healthier for us.

Thirdly, there may be a few passages which direct the course of our whole life. These will be compass points to which we return year after year. They are to us like the words of the Father to Jesus at his baptism, "You are my Son, the Beloved" (Mark 1:11). I think we may be right to imagine that these words shaped the whole life and ministry of Jesus from that point onwards. I think he may have recalled them when he was praying alone on various occasions. I have already said that I think this was the reason why he addressed God as "Abba" in Gethsemane. We can ask God to give us such compass points. My crucial one was given me before I knew I could ask for such things. At the age of fifteen, God called me to study his Scriptures in the words of Joshua 1:8–9: "This book of the law shall not depart out of your mouth; you shall meditate on it day and night, so that you may be careful to act in accordance with all that is written in it. For then you shall make your way prosperous, and then you shall be successful. I hereby command you: Be strong and courageous; do not be frightened or dismayed, for the LORD your God is with you wherever you go." My whole life story since that time, more than forty years, has been shaped in obedience to that call. And all the temptations and trials I experience are directed at turning me away from this one thing which God has called me to do.

The second kind of temptation – to lie, steal, cheat, and so on – is really a subset of the first. Anything which draws us away from following Jesus, from becoming more like the people we have been called to be, will in the end prevent us from fulfilling the call that God has placed on our lives. So the "little" temptations to bad humour or unkindness, just as much as the larger temptations to selfishness or crime, will all achieve the same ends. If we do not resist them in the name of Jesus, they will undermine our discipleship and prevent us playing our part in God's kingdom.

Standing on Christ who is beneath us

The invitation to walk in the footsteps of Jesus could be overwhelming, once we have thought about what it means, but the image of Christ surrounding us on every side encourages us to remember that we also need to rely on him. When the way is rough and uncertain, we remember that we can pray "Christ beneath me", and that he can come to our aid: "Because he himself was tested by what he suffered, he is able to help those who are being tested"

(Hebrews 2:18). Daily, in our personal prayer, we need to ask the help of Jesus, who can be the firm ground on which we stand to resist temptation.

Conclusion

There are two related ways in which we can be helped to understand what Jesus has done for us in his wounded dying and rising. We have already thought about him as an example, which we considered in relation to 1 Peter 2:21–25. His silent, innocent suffering can release us from the "spiral of violence"[10] which renders evil for evil, since we can be so inspired by what he has done that we seek the help of the same God who strengthened him. But example by itself does not always mean that people can imitate what they see. I find a particular famous pianist inspiring, but her example alone will not make *me* a good pianist.

For the example of Jesus to do more than inspire us, he needs to have done more than merely show us how he can behave. There is another kind of example, which we find in the world around and which Christians have understood Jesus to be, and that is the example of those who show us *how to do it*. The first person to climb a hitherto unconquered face of a dangerous mountain not only gives us an example of what can be done, but by discovering a feasible route also blazes a trail which makes it possible for other, less skilled, climbers to follow. In that sense, Christians have seen Jesus' life and death as an example. We call this recapitulation: at every point where Jesus could have followed the example of Adam and Eve and disobeyed God, he did something new. He turned his feet in another direction.

Until Jesus, the only examples which any human person could follow were the examples of all human persons, who, however good they might have been, were nevertheless self-centred and at times (or at all times) acting against God's call on their lives. In Jesus we now have a human example of how to live in God's way, and this example blazes the trail for us and makes it possible for us, the weaker climbers, also to walk in this way. We now know that it is possible for us to do this: "We have [a high priest] who in every respect has been tested as we are, yet without sin" (Hebrews 4:15). In the case of Jesus, our trailblazer also reaches his hand down to help us up the most challenging slopes.

You may think this does not quite explain all that Jesus has done for us, and you would be right. But it is part of the picture, and a part which fits with the theme of following in the footsteps of Jesus. His exemplary death can save us from heading off on the wrong trails.

QUESTIONS AND IDEAS

In a group

1 Read John 13:1–17 and think about it together. Ask yourselves how you could serve one another in the practical way which Jesus asks us to do. Watch out for opportunities to do the things you have recognized as possibilities. Share them when you next meet as a group.

2 Consider whether you could wash one another's feet in this group. If not, tell one another why you think not. If you want to do this, my experience at St John's suggests that you need to agree in advance that you will do this, so that everyone can come wearing clothes that make it easy. At St John's we each bring our own towel. A large bowl, a bucket of warm water and a jug or pitcher are provided. The method we use is hygienic and simple. The first person dips the jug into the bucket and the other person holds his or her feet over the bowl. The jug of water is then poured over the feet, and the washer uses the towel of the washed person to dry the feet. (Remember you are rinsing off dust, not doing a spring-clean!) Sometimes we pray for the other person out loud or silently while we do this. The person who has had his or her feet washed then repeats the process for the next person, until all have washed one another's feet.

3 Consider whether you ever help one another to walk in the steps of Jesus. If you do, share how that is helpful. If you do not, then consider how you might do it. Agree together an occasion when you

could put this into practice. What guidelines might you need to give to one another? A group I belong to has a little pebble which we put on the coffee table when we want to tell one another something which is confidential. That is a good visual signal to everyone that the thing we are going to ask for help about – for instance, keeping our temper with a difficult boss at work – is not something that we want people to discuss outside the group.

4 How might we help one another in a way which is more like Jesus' way, so that we do not imply to people that we think we are better than they are?

By yourself

1 Read John 13:1–17 and think about it. Ask yourself how you could serve others in the practical way which Jesus asks us to do. Watch out for opportunities to do the things you have recognized as possibilities.

2 Consider whether you have ever been helped by others to walk in the steps of Jesus. If you have, think how that has been helpful. Is there anyone else you could help in this way?

3 "See from his head, his hands, his feet, sorrow and love flow mingling down." Sit in a quiet place and ask God to show you in your mind's eye the feet of Jesus on the cross. (You may find it helpful to use a picture of the cross or a crucifix as a prompt.) As you contemplate those feet, what are the things which most clearly come to mind? Make a note of them. You may then find it helpful to speak a few prayers to Jesus on these themes.

4 Pray for the armour of God to be given to you. Use the passage in Ephesians 6:10–18. Could you pray for this armour to be given to you at the beginning of every day?

5 Think back over the last day, week, month and year. What are the most persistent temptations which you experience? What helps you to resist them? What makes it easier for you to give in to them? Who can you ask to help you with these?

Something to pray about

> Almighty God,
> whose most dear Son went not up to joy
> but first he suffered pain,
> and entered not into glory before he was crucified:
> mercifully grant that we, walking in the way of the cross,
> may find it none other than the way of life and peace;
> through Jesus Christ our Lord,
> Amen.[11]

FOR FURTHER READING

A.C. Bouquet, *Everyday Life in New Testament Times*, London: Batsford, 1954.

Raymond Brown, *The Death of the Messiah*, New York: Doubleday, 1994.

Jack Dominic Crossan and Jonathan Reed, *Excavating Jesus*, New York: HarperCollins, 2001.

Jeffrey B. Gibson, *The Temptations of Jesus in Early Christianity*, Sheffield: Sheffield Academic, 1995.

K.C. Hanson and Douglas E. Oakman, *Palestine in the Time of Jesus*, Minneapolis: Augsburg Fortress Press, 1998.

Bruce J. Malina, *Windows on the World of Jesus*, Louisville, Kentucky: WJK Press, 1993.

John Christopher Thomas, "Footwashing in John 13 and the Johannine Community", JSNT Sup, 61, Sheffield: JSOT Press, 1991.

J.H. Yoder, *The Politics of Jesus*, Grand Rapids: Eerdmans, 1994.

3

HIS HANDS
HEALING AND CRUCIFIXION

His body

In order to gain a clearer picture of the world in which Jesus lived, and to understand how he both adopted and challenged the culture of his time, scholars and social historians are working on archaeology and texts from the contemporary period. Some of their work will help us to see how Jesus used his hands in everyday life.

The New Testament makes it clear that Jesus is from Nazareth. As he grew up there, that setting would have had a profound influence on the way he understood himself and his world. The village was a settlement in a kind of "bowl" on top of the Nazareth range of mountains.[1] The main route east to west across Galilee passed about four miles away.[2] Careful archaeology has been able to show that at that time it was a very small village, even though the New Testament calls it a "city". There were probably between two and four hundred people living in Nazareth, mostly Jewish peasants. It is never mentioned in contemporary documents, and the conclusion must be that it was a little-known, quiet "countryside hamlet".[3] There was a water source at one end of the village which enabled them to grow food.

The work of his hands

Nazareth was surrounded by agricultural land. This would have been used for subsistence farming, with a range of different crops. Various grains were used to make bread. Olives could be grown there, producing olive oil, and vines for wine. Bean or lentil stew would have been supplemented with fish, fruit, cheese and, on rare occasions, meat. And so we have an immediate picture of the kinds of things Jesus would have handled as a child and young man. As with all subsistence farming, hunger and even famine were constant threats, since unfavourable weather, pests and diseases or political upheaval could wipe out harvests. People did not travel far, and rarely went alone for fear of attack, so everything they needed for life was produced locally or they did not have it. Everything which has been found in the burial areas indicates that the Nazareth people of the first century were extremely poor.

Since there is no archaeological evidence of homes from this period, experts have concluded that they must have been simple buildings, unlike the well built edifices elsewhere, parts of whose ornate structures can be recovered today. So the home in which Jesus lived probably had a mud floor, walls built of local rough stones, and a roof made from wooden rafters and thatch. There were also caves in Nazareth in which things could be stored, although on occasion homes were built onto them, so that the caves formed part of the living space. There was probably little public architecture in Nazareth at Jesus' time, although we know there was a synagogue. Most buildings would have been homes.

Although peasant houses were made with undressed stones, which were plentiful, they needed dressed stone at the doorway so that the doors could be hung – and this was skilled work which Jesus might well have learned to do.[4] We know that Jesus was part of an artisan's family, and his hands would therefore have been used to handle wood and other heavy material all his adult life. Archaeology has discovered some remaining door thresholds made of stone which show us that there were usually two doors, opening inwards. Because of a system of grooves in the threshold, they could only be opened a little way without being lifted, and the lifting was only possible from within the house. This gave householders some security, because they could open the door a crack to discover who was outside, before deciding whether or not to open it fully. Engaged in constructing these and other necessities, Jesus' hands were used to dirty work long before they became wet and grimy from the water in which he washed his disciples' feet. His hands were rough from such work, and perhaps had hardly any fingerprint, just like the builders who work with brick and stone today.

A most interesting story is told by the fourth-century Church historian Eusebius, in which he describes an interrogation by the Roman Emperor Domitian of the grandsons of Jude, the brother of Jesus. They were being questioned because they were descendants of David, and there was a fear of any challenge to those in power. Eusebius writes:

> He asked them how much they possessed and how much money they controlled. They said that between the two of them they possessed nine thousand denarii, half each, and they said that they did not have this in cash but that this was only the value of their twenty-five acres of land, on which they paid taxes and lived on by manual labour. *Then as testimony of their labor, they showed him their hands and hardness of bodies, with*

91

calloused hands from incessant work . . . Upon this
Domitian did not condemn them but despised them as
worthless, and released them and ordered an end to the
persecution against the church.[5]

We do not know whether Jesus helped out at harvest
time in Nazareth, although it is possible that he did, but we
do know that his teaching reflected the agriculture of the
time, with which he was clearly familiar. Living in that envi-
ronment, he would have shared the work of his time, so
that his hands alone would vividly have told the story of
his life's work.

Social customs

The social life of the time was characterized by two features which differ markedly from what we are accustomed
to in the West today. First, it is likely that Jesus and his family kept the Jewish laws of purification, which involved regular ritual hand-washing. Later in his teaching he had some
observations about this (Mark 7:1–4), and did not always
follow the laws (Luke 7:37–41), but it is likely, for instance,
that his community would have practised the rituals concerning ceremonial uncleanness after touching a dead body.

Secondly, he lived in a tactile society in which personal
space and private property were probably understood differently from the outlook prevailing in much of the current
Western world. Touching was not prohibited to friends,
because people felt that they could enter more freely what
a modern Western person would regard as their "personal
space". They probably would have walked into one
another's homes, or handled other people's property, which
in modern Western homes we would not expect people to
do, and they may well have had a more Mediterranean attitude to walking arm in arm, or embracing.

In worship, Jesus may well have lifted his hands for prayer (1 Kings 8:22, 54), clapped in praise (Psalm 47:1) and been used to people laying hands on one another in blessing (Genesis 48:17). We must remember that these hands lifted in worship were also used to the ordinary things of life – to folding clothes, to touching animals, to warm sun and blustery wind or rain, to playing games and to kindling fires.

His wounds

His hands were bound

According to John's Gospel, Jesus' hands were bound from the moment of his arrest. They "arrested Jesus and bound him" (John 18:12) as soon as Judas had betrayed him. In this Gospel there is a clear contrast between the disciples, for whom Jesus pleads freedom, saying, "let these men go" (18:8), and Jesus himself, who is unceremoniously carted off. The theme of exchange is strong in this dialogue. From that moment, Jesus was at the mercy of those who had taken him captive, in order that those who followed him might be free. He chose not to use his hands to try to retaliate.

It is noticeable that the last act of the free hands of Jesus was to heal the ear of the person who had been attacked by one of Jesus' disciples, named only in John's Gospel as Peter (John 18:10). The act of healing, recorded only in Luke, holds within it a profound juxtaposition of the purposes of the three main actors at this point. "Jesus said, 'No more of this!'" His intentions were to establish peace, to offer healing, to be life-giving. "He touched his ear and healed him" (Luke 22:51). Those who came to arrest Jesus were determined to remove by force the threat which he presented to their authority. Those who were with Jesus were fearful and uncomprehending, despite Jesus' best efforts to help them come to terms with all that lay ahead of him. Peter still believed attack to be the best form of defence, so he lashed out. Jesus himself knew that key reasons for his death were to release God's healing to the world (not just to the disciples), and to protect all his disciples from evil. Rebuking the violent disciple was an important part of defending all the disciples; their only hope of safety lay in turning the other cheek, as he had already taught them (Matthew 5:39). Their only hope of safety lay in staying under the "protection" of Jesus, which he could offer them, in human terms, only if they did not behave as if they were part of a band of brigands, or, worse still, a group of terrorists planning insurrection. Finally, their only hope of safety lay in Jesus himself dying for their healing and eternal salvation. What happened to them in the next few hours was certainly important to Jesus; but more important to him was their eternal destiny, which he also had in his hands. And so his healing hands were bound, and he was led away. We can imagine that those who had taken him captive hurried and hustled him, with no regard to his comfort, through the night to the emergency trials.

Meanwhile, the disciples went their separate ways. Most fled, but Peter followed into the courtyard of the high priest (Mark 14:66). In the long hours of that night, what did the disciples make of the fact that the last words Jesus spoke to Peter were ones of rebuke? This was not the first time that the disciples were in receipt of Jesus' stern comments; challenging their thinking or their actions was part and parcel of his teaching style. Jesus was forthright in his comments and was willing to express his love for them in anger, frustration and rebuke – we might almost say wrath. One writer on this subject helpfully allows us to see that anger is not an alternative to love, but is a way of expressing love. Those whom we love most are most able to annoy us, so our wrath flares most strongly against them. Those whom we love little, we do not bother to confront. Anger or wrath is "a mode of connectedness".[6] Jesus was deeply connected to his disciples, and he especially wanted to enable Peter to understand what was happening and to act rightly, since he was to lead the others in the days after Jesus had departed from them. So even at this stage he corrected Peter: "Jesus said to Peter, 'Put your sword back into its sheath. Am I not to drink the cup that the Father has given me?'" (John 18:11). Once again, Peter is given to understand that Jesus is adamant about his destiny.[7] The rebuke is accompanied by an act which confirms Jesus' intention to save and heal all, as he restores the ear of the man wounded by Peter. Matthew gives us to understand that this is not Jesus making the best of a difficult set of circumstances; he actively consents to be arrested. "Then Jesus said to him, 'Put your sword back into its place; for all who take the sword will perish by the sword. Do you think that I cannot appeal to my Father, and he will at once send me more than twelve legions of angels?'" (Matthew 26:52–53). The great effort Jesus expended in Gethsemane to align himself totally to the Father's will is soon bearing fruit.

There is rebuke, too, for those who came to arrest him at night, when he had been in the temple during the day and could have been captured at any time. His opponents, of course, had been determined to act in a manner which avoided any popular protest at their actions. Earlier in the week, "they wanted to lay hands on him at that very hour, but they feared the people" (Luke 20:19).

In Mark's Gospel, the binding of Jesus is mentioned later in the story, before he is taken away to Pilate (Mark 15:1). There is no reason to think that this contradicts what is found in John's Gospel. All underline, at different stages in the account, that Jesus was being treated like any other common criminal.

As we think about this part of the narrative, we should pause to consider the feeling of vulnerability experienced by anyone who has been bound. Although we may not often use our hands or arms to defend ourselves, it is nevertheless the case that uneven ground, or the apparent threat of something falling on us, will automatically cause us to lift our hands or arms to protect our faces, even when we are among friends. Our own personal experience may be confined to having an arm in a sling after an accident. Even so, we can remember the feeling of helplessness that it brings – although that is nothing in comparison to what Jesus endured. Jesus was surrounded by those who wished him ill, and in due course was to be assaulted physically as well as verbally. He stood throughout these events, bound and unable to defend himself in any way. His defencelessness is a key point of contact for any who have themselves been abused or held at the mercy of others. God turns the course of human history not through an act of defensive strength, such as "all hands to the pumps" in a boat during a storm, but through the helpless susceptibility of a man whose bound hands meant he was incapable of defending himself or even helping others.

Part of the imagery of these last events in Jesus' life is that he was bound like a lamb ready for sacrifice, and in his decision not to resist this arrest we see his active embrace of the vocation to be the Lamb of God who takes away the sin of the world (John 1:29). In the millennium display *Seeing Salvation* at London's National Gallery, there was a picture of a lamb by Fransicso de Zurbaran prepared for sacrifice that portayed the defenceless animal passively awaiting its slaughter ("The Bound Lamb"). In some ways, that picture portrays the significance of this moment more clearly than any depictions of the scene involving Jesus himself.

Christians have often seen this as a fulfilment of the Old Testament story of Abraham believing he had been commanded by God to offer his only son, Isaac, as a sacrifice. Leaving behind the servants who had accompanied them on the journey, "Abraham took the wood of the burnt-offering and laid it on his son Isaac, and he himself carried the fire and the knife . . . Isaac said to his father Abraham, '. . .The fire and the wood are here, but where is the lamb for the burnt-offering?' Abraham said, 'God himself will provide the lamb for a burnt-offering. . .'" (Genesis 22:6–8). Only after Abraham had built the altar, laid on it the wood and his bound son, and raised his knife to kill Isaac, did he hear God speak and see a ram caught in a thicket. This narrative has many resonances with the passion narrative, but one of the most significant points to note is that it is God who provides the sacrifice. We may say the same about the bound hands of Jesus: this is God himself, in his Son, providing the sacrifice which saves us from death.

His hands were forced to carry the crossbeam

Before Jesus was forced to carry the cross, his hands may also have been fixed to a whipping post to prevent him running away from the cruel flogging he endured. Already weakened by this scourging, Jesus was presented with his crossbeam. We may imagine it being thrust into his hands, or him stooping down with bleeding back and arms to lift the heavy wood onto his already disfigured shoulders:

". . .and carrying the cross by himself, he went out. . ." (John 19:17). The weight and distance were too much for him, however, and so Simon of Cyrene carried the crossbeam part of the way for Jesus.

His hands were nailed

Arriving at the place of crucifixion, the soldiers were ready to fix Jesus to the crossbeam before using forked props to hoist him up into the upright pole's notch. The Gospels do not give us very much detail at this point. As we have seen, criminals were either tied or nailed to the crossbeam, but we conclude from the description of the risen Jesus with Thomas that Jesus was nailed, since he offers his hands and side for Thomas to see (John 20:25, 27), and indeed offers his hands and feet to the disciples in the resurrection scene recorded by Luke (24:39). Although there is reference to the hands in both accounts, and this is what Christian art often portrays, it is likely that nails through the palms would not support the full weight of the body, since Jesus would move and struggle in his agony, and it might be possible for the hands to be torn away from the wood of the cross. It is more likely, therefore, that the nails went through the wrists, since for a brief period, as he was being lifted up, his body would hang completely by the wrist fixings to the crossbeam.

As we see Jesus' hands nailed to the cross, we may think of them extended in welcome, as so often in his life, or held out in a gesture of blessing and healing, or uplifted in prayer. All these themes mingle in three sayings recorded in John's Gospel which help us to understand the significance of Jesus' death.

First, Jesus himself made clear that if he was to be lifted up, he would draw all people to himself (John 12:32) – so his hands are outstretched in welcome.

Secondly, his being lifted up is comparable to the bronze serpent in the wilderness, which was provided by Moses at God's command so that the people who were afflicted with potentially lethal snake bites could look at the uplifted image and be healed (John 3:14; cf. Numbers 21:1–9). The people had been impatient with God, and were afflicted with serpents; but then in desperation they asked Moses to pray for them. This is a significant comparison which gives a further basis for thinking that the death of Jesus was also to be healing. It is difficult to judge whether the author of the fourth Gospel meant to attribute this saying to Jesus or not, so it is impossible to say whether it was part of Jesus' own understanding of the purpose of his death that it should be healing. The Gospel of John certainly supports the idea that if people turned to Jesus they would be healed, and cites Isaiah 6:10 as an explanation of why more people did not do so (John 12:40). So we may think of the outstretched hands of Jesus blessing with healing those who look to him crucified.

Thirdly, we may think of the saying, "Very truly, I tell you, unless a grain of wheat falls into the earth and dies, it remains just a single grain; but if it dies, it bears much fruit" (John 12:24), as a parallel to the serpent saying and the "lifted up" saying. His crucified hands could also be understood as uplifted in prayer, for he is offering up his life so that, in the same way as a seed dies to become abundantly fertile, his death can bear much fruit.

His life – healing and crucifixion

How were the hands of Jesus prepared for the binding and nailing which they were to endure? We have already noted the likelihood that he had lived a life in which determination to complete a task was an essential part of surviving poverty. Perhaps that was what was behind his reply to a volunteer disciple: "Jesus said to him, 'No one who puts a hand to the plough and looks back is fit for the kingdom of God'" (Luke 9:62). Hard manual work requires a degree of persistence which brings about certain character traits. But there are some other things described in the Gospels which may help us to understand how Jesus could open his hands and let go of life, possessions, family and friends, as well as all acts of violence, in this decisive self-offering.

His hands were used to receive

Jesus is able to give all this up because he knows that his Father "has placed all things in his hands", because "the Father loves the Son" (John 3:35). In the context of such love, which both accepts and trusts him with the future of all things, Jesus is able to give away such "little things" as he has in his earthly life for the sake of the promised outcome. Only hands which are full can become empty.

His hands were used to bless

Full of the Father's blessing himself, Jesus is able to bless others, commanding the disciples to "bless those who curse you" (Luke 6:28), which we presume he did during his life as well as on the cross: "Father, forgive them; for they do not know what they are doing" (Luke 23:34). Already in this action we see Jesus giving away the love of God to people without discrimination. The disciples are reluctant to worry him with the children, but Jesus is willing to take the trouble to lay hands on them and pray (Matthew 19:13–15). In Mark the description makes it clear that "people were bringing little children to him in order that he might touch them", but the disciples "spoke sternly to them". This produces in Jesus an indignant response, because "it is to such as these that the kingdom of God belongs" (Mark 10:13–16). Although there is rhythm in the ministry of Jesus, of withdrawal to pray or to teach the disciples followed by public ministry, there is no sense of self-protection when he is faced with those who are seeking God. The fact that some of these children are infants (Luke 18:15) does not make Jesus think that this is a waste of time or energy; he expresses entirely the kingdom values which he teaches. As he blesses, he also opens the disciples to the possibility that children matter as much as, if not more than, adults, and thereby reconciles different age groups to one another, teaching them that they belong to one another in the kingdom.

His hands were used to share

On several occasions in the Gospel narratives, Jesus' hands were the focus of everyone's attention as he blessed and broke bread. This is first described at the feeding of the multitudes, when the child's five barley loaves and two fish became enough to feed 5,000 (John 6:1–14). This is much more than an acted parable, but it nevertheless shows that the teaching of Jesus about sharing with those in need (Luke 6:30–31) was also something which he practised. We are so used to reading such stories that we do not always notice that his hands are not used to hold onto things for himself. It would be laughable to try to imagine Jesus saying in response to Andrew's discovery of the child with the bread, "Oh well, at least *we* need not go hungry!"

Jesus' hands were also used to bless, break and share the bread at the final supper he had with his disciples (Mark 14:22–25). On that occasion his intention was certainly to teach his disciples what they were to expect in the next hours. As they received symbols of his brokenness from his own hands, they were invited to embrace brokenness for themselves. These acts of sharing began the establishment of a community which was soon engaged in a radical sharing of possessions and gifts (see Acts 2:44; 4:32–36).

His hands were used to heal

Many times we read that Jesus laid hands on or touched a person, and that person was healed. Jairus' daughter, for instance, was presumed dead by her grieving relatives, but Jesus simply took her by the hand and was able to restore her alive to her parents (Matthew 9:25). The woman who had been crippled for eighteen years by a spirit and who "was bent over and . . . quite unable to stand up straight" (Luke 13:11) recovered immediately when Jesus laid hands on her. On one occasion, Jesus used his hands to make a paste with his own saliva and mud before he healed the man who had been blind since birth (John 9:6). On many occasions the touch of Jesus was a crucial part of the way in which the power of God worked to bring healing to a variety of ailments, all of which were severely handicapping the persons concerned.

On two occasions at least, Jesus was willing to touch when the religious rules of the time prohibited contact if at all possible, since to touch would be to become ceremonially unclean. The first was when he was approached by "a man covered with leprosy" (Luke 5:12–16). There was no known cure at that time, so human wisdom kept such people from coming close to others for fear of contagion. Jesus, however, feared neither the religious rules, nor the possibility of being infected. His compassion for the person made him "stretch out his hand" to touch him. The touch and command of Jesus brought healing and cleansing to this sufferer. Secondly, Jesus' sympathy led him to reach out his hand to touch and stop the bier of a young man whose funeral he encountered in Nain. He immediately recognized that the widow, having lost her only son, was likely to be destitute now that she had no one to provide for her. Jesus commanded the man to stand and, we must assume, took him by the hand, since Luke says that he "gave him to his mother" (Luke 7:11–17). In each case, Jesus' willingness to touch and heal resulted in the person being restored to their community. Healing people's bodies also meant restoring their social relationships. Healing is never a matter of physical healing alone; it always touches the whole person.

There are other stories where, in similar ways, Jesus brings healing to others. He was fearless in touching those who were sick or afflicted by evil spirits, or who had died. Those whom others would not be in contact with, or whom they would try to avoid, Jesus was willing to touch. Hands that did not fear what others avoided were also prepared to embrace the cross and to endure its suffering.

His hands were used to hanging on until the job was done

Three things suggest that Jesus was capable of taking a firm hold. First, he is recorded as "making a whip of cords" so that he could drive out of the temple those who were using it not as a place of prayer, but as a kind of cattle market, selling animals for sacrifice, and also as a kind of bank, exchanging Roman coins carrying the offensive image of Caesar for the local Jewish coins (John 2:13–22). Jesus "drove all of them out of the temple" and overturned the tables of the money-changers. Thus he restored the possibility of ordinary people being able to come into relationship with God without the intervening extortion of those who would make it difficult for them. Challenging the customs of his time, he was fearless before those over whom his social position gave him no authority. Such a hands-on approach, his disciples later reflected, had set him on course towards the cross.

On another occasion he was equally determined, but in this setting was not to be rushed into any precipitate action. A woman was brought to him, accused of adultery, and he twice bent down and wrote in the dust to buy time until her accusers (and his) slunk away, outmanoeuvred by Jesus' reply: "Let anyone among you who is without sin be the first to throw a stone at her" (John 8:1–11). His calm handling of the affair saved her from certain death, and also saved his reputation as the friend of sinners who also upheld, indeed strengthened, the law of God as it had been received in the Old Testament. The woman was restored to the community from which she would have been ostracized, and was given the chance to live in a new way by his merciful call to sin no more.

Finally, both of these stories well illustrate a saying of Jesus, the good shepherd: "No one will snatch them [my sheep] out of my hand" (John 10:28). Whether it is the people who want to pray in the temple, or the woman at the centre of an elaborate plot to trick Jesus, they are safe in his hands. He will use his hands to protect the vulnerable, to heal the untouchables. His defence of them is unassailable, although it will turn out that his hands will suffer in their protection.

What does this mean for us as a faith community?

Letting our hands bless the communities in which we live

Many Christians in the West are discovering that where the Church seems to be rather distant from its context, the reason is often because it has forgotten to serve its neighbours. Some of the strongest churches are ones where people are building regular service to the community into the pattern of their lives, individually and as a community, on a weekly or monthly basis. This may happen through small fellowship groups not only reading the Bible and praying together (which can become a fairly safe and self-indulgent activity), but also taking time to do acts of practical love for people who may have no understanding of the faith. This will always be costly of both time and effort, but can be very rewarding. Its costliness reminds us that the hands of blessing which Jesus stretched out were pierced, and we must expect to carry the scars of the God-given love which we pour out.

Being communities of reconciliation

One of the hardest questions which I find myself forced to answer is this: how can I preach the gospel of reconciliation if I am not in a reconciled relationship with others? I came slowly and painfully to the conclusion that I could not do so while I held any sense of enmity against others.

The question first struck me when I was elected to the Church of England's General Synod. There I found that not only did I disagree with a large number of members, but some were engaged in ways of behaving which seemed to me clearly contrary to the gospel. (I am sure they saw the same in me!) The Church at that time was grappling with the difficult issue of whether to ordain women as priests, and alongside that debate there were also personal animosities which were far in excess of anything I had experienced before.

And so I found myself plunged into this uneasy atmosphere, and called of God to try to live the reconciliation which I believed was at the heart of the gospel. One of the questions was how to live this in a way which did not dodge the issues that separated us, and did not perpetuate the dysfunctional relationships that so often seemed to prevail. I am not claiming that I discovered any final answer to this, but I did find some things to be very important.

First, there was a need to pray for those with whom I did not agree. Intercession, I discovered, seemed to make a difference in both the one praying and the one prayed for. Secondly, there was the important task of really attending to the arguments of those who disagreed with me, so that I could understand their views properly. Thirdly, it always helped if we could simultaneously deal with matters on which we did agree and could stand together in our common humanity or in our common Christian faith. And finally, there was the task of disagreeing fully and frankly, in a way which took the other viewpoint seriously enough to engage with it and to respond in courtesy.

Somehow there were some people of the opposite view with whom I formed a deepening fellowship, even while the debate was fiercest. That was a blessing to me. I learned a good deal from them, and valued their friendship in the

Lord. This seemed to me to take a great deal of courage on both sides – the kind of courage which our Lord displayed in allowing his hands to be stretched out on the cross. Often it felt safer not to speak to those with whom I did not agree; it was easier to maintain the distinctions to which I and my colleagues were wedded if I did not take the time to understand the arguments of those we opposed. It was more comfortable to surround ourselves with those who would not challenge our arguments. But the validity of the gospel is called into question every time we do not honour those whose lives Jesus took so seriously that he was willing to die for them. The call to preach a gospel of love is violated every time we refuse to love all those with whom we have violent disagreements, since our love is to be for enemy as well as for friend. It is not the case that the responsibility for reconciling relationships belongs only to those who have formal ministerial responsibility. It belongs to all Christians, and we remember that Jesus had a strong warning for those who would not forgive their enemies: they could kiss goodbye to the forgiveness of God (Matthew 18:23–35).

Since this time, the national and international Church has been facing other equally divisive questions. We cannot walk away from each other, since we are told that we are members together of the household of faith and have a responsibility for one another. Neither must we misrepresent one another, as it is so easy to do. We owe it to one another to listen carefully and to take one another seriously enough to experience the pain of hearing differing viewpoints and understanding them. Only then can we search together for God's way forward.

Such a search for reconciliation over issues is echoed by the need to seek for reconciliation between the churches.

We live in an age in which there has been unprecedented progress towards a resolution of inherited theological divisions, but in which Church unity is still a long way off. As old differences are resolved, new ones spring up. And yet, we know that if we are to engage in effective mission, this can only be done where there is significant collaboration, and a determination to reject self-seeking so that the gospel can be given into every section of society. Where church leaders and church communities are reconciled, God blesses them and those to whom they minister: "How very good and pleasant it is when kindred live together in unity! . . . there the LORD ordained his blessing, life for evermore" (Psalm 133:1, 3).

Letting the reconciliation of the Church flow out to society

When Christians are bidden to pray for the welfare of the city where they live, I think that includes acting in its best interests. Two examples of what this might mean have been seen in recent Christian history. First, the Christian churches in South Africa were very active in the period immediately before the fall of apartheid. Their commitment to reconciliation in the gospel precipitated their search for a way forward that would avert bloodshed in the tinderbox of the divided society in which they had all been forced to live. Archbishop Desmond Tutu's work on the Truth and Reconciliation Commission may well have averted much violence. We do well to pray that other nations will also have such visionaries to bring about reconciliation.

Secondly, there are those who have been quietly building bridges between different groups in UK society, so that when international tensions grow, they do not issue in vio-

lence on the streets of our inner cities, where vastly differing cultures are represented. I understand that there are
some nights when leaders of reconciliation walk the streets
of their cities trying to disperse crowds of inflamed people
who are looking for an occasion to initiate violence.

What does this mean for us personally?

Receiving Christ's healing in ourselves

"By his bruises we are healed" (Isaiah 53:5). Christians
have understood this verse in a variety of ways, but nearly all
have associated it with the wounds Jesus bore on the cross.
Some have taken it to refer only to the "healing of sin",
assuming it to be a way of saying that our forgiveness, which
is a kind of spiritual healing, comes from the work of Jesus on
the cross. Others have taken it to mean that when the
Church prays for healing, it is recognizing that what Jesus
achieved on the cross was far greater than simply dealing
with sin, so that any healing we pray for and receive is the
result of the grace of God made available to us through Jesus'
death. Such a view does not regard healing as automatic, but
as something which is within the sovereign disposal of God.
Such healing is an overflow of the death of Jesus, since it was
the fall of Adam which brought sickness into the world, and
it is the reversal of that fall which Jesus has achieved on the
cross. Others trace a very clear view that if the death of Jesus
has really reversed all the effects of the fall, then that means
Christians can claim now all the benefits of his passion, so
that healing is ours by right – it is our inheritance. This has
given rise to a view which has been summarized as "name it
and claim it", by which we can name all the things which
have been achieved at the cross and then claim them. Such

a view cannot tolerate that any Christians will not be healed – and so lack of healing is blamed on a lack of faith in the sick person, or on a lack of faith in the person praying for them, or on too much reliance on drugs or medical assistance.

There would be very few Christians over the last two thousand years who have denied that people can ever be healed by God in response to prayer. In the modern West, however, there has been very little expectation that people would be healed directly by God, and so much praying is for those who are using contemporary medical methods, rather than allowing the possibility that sometimes God may heal directly. By contrast, Christians in other parts of the world have never lost the sense of expectation which the early Church had that God would sometimes heal directly. Most Christians have also recognized that before the second coming of Jesus, for all Christians, death can be the last great healing in our lives. It can be our final act of self-surrender in trustful reliance on God. And it can be God's final healing of our sin and our sickness, relieving us from the habits of the former and the suffering of the latter.

I believe that in the cross of Jesus God deals with much more than individual sin, although he certainly does deal with that there. There is no biblical basis for the belief that God intended the miracles which Jesus performed to cease until he came again. As an Anglican I do not feel obliged to believe anything which cannot be grounded in Scripture, so I hold to the view that in the cross of Jesus God dealt with all that was contrary to his purposes for creation, but we will not fully see what that means until the end time. While we live in the time between the cross and the second coming – when everything has been changed because of the cross, but has not all been completed – we are forgiven all that we repent, but not yet finally freed from the sinful

world as we will be at the end time. And so it is with healing. We are still part of a suffering world in which sickness
and death are plentiful, and yet sometimes the healing
power of God which was released on the cross is poured
out in miraculous healings. As surely as we can believe that
at the end time we will be finally forgiven, so we can
believe that we will be finally healed when Jesus comes
again and we receive our resurrection bodies.

This view allows that God's sovereignty means he may
heal in all manner of different ways; that it is always right
to pray for healing, but never right to demand it or suggest
to others that God denies it because of their or our inad-
equacy. God is healing the whole created order through the
cross of Jesus, and that includes our current humanity.
Although its final healing will be at the resurrection, we
sometimes have an anticipation of that end time, as we do
by the reception of the Holy Spirit who is the seal to assure
us of what is to come (Ephesians 1:13–14).

You may be wondering why it is that sin is always forgiven because of the cross, but other benefits are not automatically received. I think we can best understand this if
we remember that forgiveness restores our relationship to
God, which is the foundation of all that follows. Every
Christian receives the Holy Spirit, but the manner in which
the gifts of the Spirit and the fruit of the Spirit are given
takes account of the individual's circumstances. Perhaps
receiving healing is more like receiving the Holy Spirit than
receiving forgiveness. God is healing us, but the way he does
that and the timescale are entirely within his sovereign gift,
whereas he has committed himself to giving forgiveness to
all who turn to Christ.

Forgiveness is an anticipation of the final verdict on the
day of judgment, just as healing is an anticipation of what

will be ours at the end time. Any healing which we receive now, however miraculous (and I believe that it is sometimes indeed that), is not to our resurrection body, which will be our final healing. So it is now and not yet, and we have to trust God's providential care that allows some of us part of the healing we desire, while allowing others to move through death to the healing which he will give at the end time. That we will be finally healed is entirely due to the work of Jesus on the cross, and any anticipation of that healing is welcomed as a sign of the fuller healing which is to come.

In response to all this we need to open our hands to his nail-pierced hands, to receive all the healing that he wishes to give to us, whether it be spiritual, physical, mental or emotional.

Offering Christ's healing to others

This may be something new to you, or it may be the case that you have been part of a Christian fellowship which has had long experience in this area. Those who follow Jesus need to learn to stretch out their hands as willingly as he did to all kinds of people so that they may also receive his grace. There are three ways in which we may do this, described below. All of them are modelled on the ministry of Jesus.

Hands of thanksgiving and blessing

When we pray for others that they may receive God's healing, it is often the case that we need to begin by thanking God for the person for whom we pray, before we ask for God's blessing. The kind of pattern we might adopt is the one we see at the end of the mission of the Seventy, when "Jesus rejoiced in the Holy Spirit and said, 'I thank you, Father, Lord of heaven and earth, because you have hidden these things from the wise and the intelligent . . . yes, Father, for such was your gracious will'" (Luke 10:21). Hearing of the work which the disciples had done, Jesus gave thanks for the way in which God had acted in and through them.

This seems to me to be important for two reasons. First, it turns our eyes on God, and reminds us of what he has done already, so it builds our faith. Some years ago, in North America, I was asked to lead a service in a place where they were unaccustomed to praying in this kind of way, and one could feel that the congregation did not expect God to be very active. We needed first to turn our attention to him, before we were strong enough even to think of picking up the needs of those among us who were sick and struggling. When we look around us at the immense needs of the world, it is easy to be discouraged. When we fix our eyes on God, we are reminded that this is the Creator of the universe who has raised our Lord Jesus Christ from the dead; for him all things are possible (Luke 1:37).

The second reason why it is so important to thank God for the people who are before us for prayer (whether they are there in our imagination or in the same time and place as us) is that we need our hearts to be full of love for them, in order to pray effectively. So we might thank God for the people he has made them to be, and for all that they have been and done so far. There might be things they have done for us for which we can thank God. When I pray for individuals in front of me I often know enough about them to make this quite an extensive prayer. When I pray for Sudanese Christians suffering persecution again, I can at least thank God for their faith and their courage in the face of such opposition.

113

When I have thanked God for who he is and who he has made this person or persons to be, then I am ready to ask God to bless them, with all the mercies which the New Testament often describes. If I use my hands in prayer, and I often do, then I can hold them palms up in thanksgiving and palms down in blessing – in the way adults do with children they know, putting an affirming hand on their head or shoulder. In my tradition, it is customary only for priests to pronounce blessings over people. In the Old Testament and in some other Christian traditions, however, all people are thought to be able to give a blessing to another person, and occasionally you will hear people asking if they have someone's blessing to act in some way or another. I am sure that God does not withhold his blessing from anyone when a Christian prays that another may receive it, so whatever our tradition we may pray God's blessing on others.

Hands of intercession for the sick

When we have thanked God and asked his blessing on someone, it may then be the case that this person is sick and needs our intercessory prayers. If we are praying for people at a distance, we may not know all the details of their current needs, but God knows better than anyone else, so we do not have to worry about telling God all the details. Our prayer will be that God will send his Holy and healing Spirit into the lives of these people, to bring them a sense of his presence, a greater trust in him, and healing of body, mind and spirit.

If we do not know quite how to pray for someone because he or she is close to death and we think that it may be the moment when God will take that person to himself, or if we simply cannot find the words, then it may help to use our hands, through our imagination, in another way.

Remembering that four people put their sick friend on a mat and carried him to Jesus, breaking through the roof because there were so many other people in the house, we may be able to imagine doing just that – carrying our friend to Jesus. In one sense, that is what prayer is. And it is all we need to do, since, in the Gospel story, the rest happened between Jesus and the sick person. The friends may have thought that the most pressing need was to heal his paralysis. Jesus knew better, and dealt first with his sin. That is why we can ask for healing in every part, and be sure that God will answer our prayers, even if not in the ways which we expect (Mark 2:1–12).

Laying hands on the sick

Whether or not you are familiar with this, we need to acknowledge that Jesus often touched the sick people who were brought to him. It seems also to have been the frequent custom of the early Church (Acts 3:7; 20:10), and it is directly recommended by one of the New Testament writers (James 5:14). As an evangelical, it was this last command which took me through a "pain barrier" of reluctance to venture laying hands on people, when we began the practice in our local church of praying for and anointing the sick. Our minister believed that we should do this, and invited me to assist. With very little faith and even less expectation that anything much would happen, I accepted his invitation out of obedience to God's word. Years later, I am still amazed at the ways in which God answers these prayers. For years I found it hard to admit that this was happening, but a student at college made me face the truth. His gentle ragging of me about what happened when, with others, I prayed, laid hands on and anointed people made me acknowledge that God did indeed do unexpected things today, just as he did in the time of Jesus.

Conclusion

A number of key passages in the New Testament suggest that the cross of Jesus is crucial for reconciliation between human beings and God, or between human beings themselves. Although these are interrelated, we will think about them separately at first. Extolling the wonder and grace of God in Christ, St Paul writes in conclusion, "Through him God was pleased to reconcile to himself all things, whether on earth or in heaven, by making peace through the blood of his cross" (Colossians 1:20). Such an affirmation inevitably makes us wonder why everything and everyone needed to be reconciled to God. There are a number of ways of answering this question, but the clearest concerns something we hear little about in contemporary teaching or preaching. It concerns the wrath of God.

God took the initiative to reconcile the world and its people to himself, because human sin had placed all under the wrath of God. This has been made clear in the gospel, which shows us both God's righteousness and his wrath (Romans 1:17–18). Paul explains that "the wrath of God is revealed from heaven against all ungodliness and wickedness of those who by their wickedness suppress the truth" (Romans 1:18). We are used to thinking of wrath or anger as a human emotion which often overwhelms a person so that he or she is incapable of acting rationally, and which precludes other more positive attitudes being held simultaneously by the person who is angry. Both these assumptions can mislead us when we think about God. Since God is not human, we must not assume that when God's wrath is described it means that he is irrational or out of control. His anger, unlike most human anger, is righteous, which means that it is justified – there is good cause and the response of wrath is proportional to the cause. But it is also the case that God's anger never excludes his love. Despite human sin which justly deserved God's implacable opposition, that is his wrathful response, he "so loved the world that he gave his only Son, so that everyone who believes in him may not perish but may have eternal life" (John 3:16).

It seems that it is possible for God to be utterly opposed to human sinfulness, and for the unrepentant to stand under his wrath, even while he loves them so much that he is willing to become human himself in Jesus Christ, in order to turn them back to himself so that they can be reconciled with him. Paul describes it in this way: "We are convinced that one has died for all; therefore all have died. And he died for all, so that those who live might live no longer for themselves, but for him who died and was raised for them ... All this is from God, who reconciled us to himself through Christ, and has given us the ministry of reconciliation" (2 Corinthians 5:14–19). When we look to the cross, it is as if we see the hands of God outstretched to us, pleading that we will trust him and be reconciled to him.

It is also the case that a centuries-old division between different people groups, or lifelong separations between individuals, can be overcome in the cross of Jesus. Paul addresses a major rift in the church of his time, between the Christians who had been born into the Jewish nation and faith and those who had been born into other nations – referred to as Gentiles. For a number of reasons, these two groups had very little to do with one another. For the Jewish people, there were a number of Old Testament commands designed to keep them faithful to Yahweh, which encouraged them to avoid contact with those who worshipped other gods. Chief amongst these was the prohibition on worshipping idols, which nearly all the other nations did. But there were also a number of food laws, such as avoiding pork, as well as rules about how food was to be prepared. This made any kind of mutual hospitality very difficult. The Gentiles, for their part, did not always find it easy to understand or sympathize with the Jewish way of faith, which was so alien to their culture and beliefs.

This situation made the life of the early Church very problematic, because the early leaders were not sure whether Gentiles ought to be admitted to the Christian community at all, which was initially made up entirely of converted Jews. If Gentiles could become Christians, on what terms should this happen? Did they need to become proselytes and join the Jewish faith first? As the Church struggled with these questions, they were addressing both practical matters, such as whether they could enter one another's houses and share the bread and wine of the sup-per commanded by Jesus to be done in remembrance of him, as well as more theological questions, which were to set the course of the whole Church's life in every follow-ing century. In every stream of New Testament documents there is a strong affirmation that God's purpose is unity. This is ultimately to be the unity of the whole created order with God himself (Ephesians 1:10), but it is also the unity of all the followers of Jesus, for which we are told that Jesus prayed (John 17:11). All the commands to love fellow Christians could be taken to deal with this matter too. We will look here at a passage which specifically links unity – brought about by reconciliation – with the death of Jesus.

Ephesians 2 explicitly claims that Jesus has made the two divided people groups one in his body on the cross. Paul uses a variety of pictures to help us understand how this has been achieved. First, he depicts the Gentiles as far distant from God, while the Jewish people, who are God's covenant people, are nearer to God but still needing reconciliation, since they have failed to keep their covenants with God. The distancing from God has been overcome by the death of Jesus. Now both groups are near to God, and all barriers have been removed. Paul explains that this has happened because Jesus has fulfilled the law and thereby "abolished it". For the Jewish Christian, there is no longer any need to fulfil the food laws, for instance, so that they can draw near to God. Because the law has been fulfilled for everyone, it is also now possible for the Gentiles to be forgiven for their idolatry and they too can draw near to God. For both Jew and Gentile, all that is necessary is for them to recognize that it is "by grace you have been saved", since God incarnate in Jesus Christ has done all that is necessary for both groups. He has kept God's side of the covenant as well as our human side. The mechanism is never fully explained in this passage; we read the simple affirmation that it is "by the blood of Christ" (Ephesians 2:13).

This means that the distant people are brought near; the aliens are adopted into God's family; where the dividing wall between them has been broken down, the separate people groups have been made into one household! Jesus is our peace, because his death has made peace. By "putting to death that hostility" through the cross, he has proclaimed peace to us (Ephesians 2:16–17).

In this complex passage, images and pictures are interwoven and heaped on one another in order to make the main point clear: there is no separation for those who believe in Jesus. His death makes it possible for us all to address God as Father, by the work of the Holy Spirit, and this leads us to recognize that we are brothers and sisters in one family. We are also compared to a temple in which God dwells, so that we are being built together on the

Questions and ideas

In a group

1 Ask one of the group to read one of the following passages: Luke 22:47–53; Mark 10:13–16; Luke 7:11–17. Allow yourselves time to imagine the scene and to see Jesus use his hands in mercy. How do you want to respond to this?

2 If you can meet in a church where Jesus is depicted in a window or in some other art, or if you can use a picture of a Gospel scene you have found in a book or on the Internet, you may wish to spend some time meditating on that together, focusing on his hands. Jesus could be shown in a number of different settings – perhaps in the nativity scenes which come to us in the Christmas season, when the child's hands are depicted stretched out in longing or imploring to his mother, or in blessing-like action to the visitors. Look at the hands of Jesus as he is shown healing the sick, or reproving the rich young man. You may wish to take time to allow yourself to see the hands of Jesus stretched out towards you, or even to feel his touch of healing. Share with one another what you have noticed.

3 Most communities have division and trouble within them. Identify where that is nearest to you – in your church or in the locality where you live. Take time to think about the underlying causes. Pray for reconciliation. Help one another to think about ways in which you could act to decrease the tensions, or to bring peace.

4 Plan a service in which the ministry of healing could be offered. If you do not generally have such services, ask those who are elders or ministers whether such a service could take place.

5 Write a litany for reconciliation in the world – in Iraq, or Sudan, or Israel/Palestine, or Pakistan/India. Pray it together.

By yourself

1 Meditate on a picture of the crucifixion, or on the scene in your mind's eye, focusing on Jesus' sacred hands, and using these words from Graham Kendrick as your prompt: "Hands that flung stars into space, to cruel nails surrendered."

2 Spend some time reflecting on the way that Jesus' hands were pinned in a posture which would be natural for him – the arms stretched out in welcome, blessing and prayer. Do you find one of these more attractive than the others? Ask yourself why that is, and then ask Jesus to welcome, bless, or pray for you.

3 Read Colossians 1:3–12. Note how Paul first thanks God for all that he knows of the people to whom he writes, and then prays enormous blessing for them in verses 9–12. Think of someone for whom you want to pray. Either write a prayer in two parts like this, or speak it out loud, or quietly in your heart. Part A is a short thanksgiving for all that is good in the person for whom you want to pray. Part B is a prayer for God's abundant blessing on that person. Maybe you would like to use the exact words which Paul uses in verses 9–12.

4 Read Matthew 18:23–35 slowly. Ask yourself if you are throwing God's forgiveness away by holding onto old grievances. If you are, but find it difficult to let them go so that you can forgive the people who have wronged you, pray that God will give you the gift of his Holy Spirit of love and forgiveness so that you can release your anger and resentment and receive his forgiveness for them and for yourself.

5 Ask the Lord to give you the cross in your inmost being, so that your hands can proffer it to others as the place of healing.

A prayer for this week

O Christ the Master Carpenter,
who at the last, through wood and nails,
purchased our whole salvation,
wield well your tools in the workshop of your world,
so that we who come rough hewn to your bench
may here be fashioned to a truer beauty of your hand.
We ask it for your own name's sake,
Amen.[8]

FOR FURTHER READING

A. Campbell, *The Gospel of Anger*, London: SCPK, 1986.

Jack Dominic Crossan and Jonathan Reed, *Excavating Jesus*, New York: HarperCollins, 2001.

M. Sawicki, *Crossing Galilee*, Harrisburg, PA: Trinity Press, 2000.

HIS SIDE
TEACHING AND CRUCIFIXION

His body

Many people walked beside Jesus during his lifetime. When he was learning to walk, Mary or Joseph held his little hands while he began to put one foot in front of the other. Children played with him, and other families accompanied him and his family to Jerusalem on pilgrimage (Luke 2:41–51). He sat beside people in the synagogue and the marketplace, and at table. The stories of most of those accompanying him in the early days of his life are hidden from us; we can only guess what it might have meant for him and for them.

Families in those times were always extended families – unlike the "nuclear" families we know today in the West. In a small rural community, Jesus was probably never far away from other family members. Even his contemporaries who lived in the cities would have been physically close to an extended family, since houses often held more than one husband/wife group. Such a living arrangement produced households where there were a number of adults as well as children. Because people lived in close proximity and knew one another very well, they did not have or expect such privacy as Western homes afford today. Scholars suggest that this is why the Gospels can refer to Jesus being "alone" when there are still a few people around him (e.g. Mark

4:10; Luke 9:18). It means to be with one's closest friends or family, and not necessarily "solitary".[1]

There were two focal institutions in rural and peasant life. One was kinship through family, and the other was political through king, ruler or Caesar.[2] In Nazareth there would be no separation between family and faith. Faith was handed on through close family relationships, around the family meals. "Domestic religion seeks meaning through belonging."[3] Thus, while Jesus learned to live in family, there was another social reality, or way in which people lived alongside one another. This was expressed through social or financial power, often closely interleaved. Politics, often in the hands of powerful family groups, controlled society for the good of the powerful, at the expense of the poor. The powerful often lived in the cities and larger towns, and the poor in the small villages and rural communities. Many of the most powerful owned large estates of land on which they would also have dwellings. The powerful in the larger cities depended on a hinterland of villages and towns for their food and other staple supplies.

In this kind of society, patrons really mattered, because they might be able to supply some of the needs of those upon whose services they also depended. In such a relationship there is real mutuality, even when the parties are not equally rich or influential. The honour of the rich or powerful can be protected even when there can be no material repayment, since a village or town might make public attribution of thanks to a benefactor, perhaps in inscriptions on buildings. It seems that there were clear ways of relating which required reciprocity and also guarded honour on the part of both parties, even when the relationship existed between non-equals.

Challenging the pattern

In the society of his time, Jesus would have lived in two interrelated sets of relationships – those of family, and those of his social grouping in society, given to him by his family origins. He chose, however, to move out of this common pattern of life, setting up another group whose "being alongside" had nothing to do with blood relationships or social status. Indeed, his willingness to transgress both sets of mores set him on course for the suffering which he experienced in his woundedness on the cross. He decided not to be defined by his family setting, and to ignore the patterns of honour which prevailed in society more widely. He was willing to include alongside him people whose family or social status made them undesirable, and to challenge the privilege of those whose family or power should have put them beyond his reach.

So after his cousin John began to preach in the wilderness, and the Spirit had led Jesus himself into the wilderness, he began his adult ministry by calling some to be alongside him throughout the time he was teaching and preaching. These people spent weeks beside him, listening, watching and learning. Others were his sponsors or familiar friends, among whom were a number of women, to whom he also related in ways which transgressed the social patterns of the time. A few, Peter, James and John, went with him when the larger group or crowds were forbidden (e.g. Mark 5:37; 9:2; 14:33). Although we know there were tensions among the disciples, there was also a new community created on the preaching-healing journeys which they undertook with Jesus and in pairs. This community was to survive the cataclysmic events of the crucifixion and resurrection, and even later persecution.

As the Gospels unfold the story, it becomes clear that Jesus had no strategic plan for reorganizing the whole of society, but it would be a mistake to imagine that society would remain the same after his death. By attracting into his company not only the Twelve, but also many other disciples, some influential Jewish leaders such as Joseph of Arimathea, and the rich women who patronized his mission, together with outcast peoples such as lepers and tax collectors, Jesus began the process of drawing alongside him – and thereby alongside one another – people who belong together in the kingdom of God, where family and social status are disregarded in the light of their new relationship to him, which is one of "friends" (John 15:15). Friends of Jesus do not refuse to associate with Samaritans (John 4:7ff.), Syro-Phoenicians (Mark 7:24–30), children, women, slaves, the ritually unclean, the possessed. None of the usual definitions seem to be significant when once they have learned that they are all to call God "Abba" and recognize that they are all in their different ways gifts to Jesus from the Father (John 17:6).

It is no wonder that Jesus' teaching makes radical calls for different attitudes which no longer allow money, outward position or gender to be the defining criteria for being alongside one another. People who gathered about Jesus were electing to reorder their commitments to family, and hence to their social or political groups. Scholars have suggested that in some ways they were more like city groups of artisans who freely elected to cooperate, although these were far narrower in their compass, of course, than the disciples of Jesus. Deciding to be "alongside" Jesus turned out to be an act which radically rearranged family relationships and social position. Some who had been "in" socially or politically would be excluded because of their association

FRIDAY

All the Kingdoms of the World *Malcolm Guite*

So here's the deal and this is what you get:
The penthouse suite with world-commanding views,
The banker's bonus and the private jet,
Control and ownership of all the news,
An 'in' to that exclusive one per cent,
Who know the score, who really run the show,
With interest on every penny lent
And sweeteners for cronies in the know.
A straight arrangement between me and you,
No hell below or heaven high above,
You just admit it, and give me my due,
And wake up from this foolish dream of love …
But Jesus laughed, 'You are not what you seem.
Love is the waking life, you are the dream.'

Then the devil led him up and showed him in an instant all the
kingdoms of the world. And the devil said to him, 'To you I will
give their glory and all this authority; for it has been given over
to me and I give it to anyone I please. If you, then, will worship
me, it will all be yours.' (Luke 4.5–7)

with Jesus, while others who were socially excluded would be included in the kingdom of God by their relationship with Jesus. We may think of it like a game of draughts or chess: one piece is moved which does not physically change the location of all the other pieces, but it changes all their interrelationships.

His wounds

The wound in the side of Jesus is mentioned only in John's Gospel, as are several other features of the last week of Jesus' life, such as the foot-washing. This wound is inflicted on the body of Jesus after he has died. In John's narrative, the crucifixion takes place on the day of preparation for the Passover, and it was therefore desirable to lay the body of Jesus in a tomb before everything stopped for the festival in the early evening. There would have been a yearning on the part of the disciples not to allow any further dishonour to their beloved teacher, but Jewish law also forbade leaving bodies exposed after dusk and that would have been augmented by the fact that the next day was the Sabbath (Deuteronomy 21:22–23).

Jesus had only been hanging on the cross for a few hours, and since some crucified people took two or three days to die, there was obviously a concern on the part of the authorities to ensure that he really had died. In the event, they received that assurance, but not because they had concurred with the malevolent request of the Jewish authorities to break the victim's legs. Several things could have contributed to this swift demise. First, Jesus was flogged before he was executed, and Roman floggings were sometimes sufficient alone to kill. (I have already explained that it was possible that there were two floggings, which would have weakened him even more.) Secondly, he was nailed rather than lashed to the cross, and so would have been bleeding from yet more open wounds. On this occasion, the desire to remove the bodies of the three crucified men meant that the soldiers began to crush the legs of the victims, which hastened death by making it impossible for them to breathe, since their whole body slumped forward. It also meant that, should they somehow survive, there could be no escape after they had been taken down from the cross. But there was no need to break Jesus' legs.

His side was pierced

They were surprised to find that Jesus had already died, but in order to guarantee that this was really the case, a soldier pierced his side. The verb used can describe both a prodding to make sure that the victim really is dead, or a deep plunging into the heart to finish him off.[4] Whether it means that the lance was used to prick or to thrust in, to arouse a person who has fainted, or to sink deeply into the dead body, it was certainly the soldier's intention to ensure that Jesus made no reaction and was really dead.

We have no way of knowing which side of Jesus' body was pierced, since the Gospels do not tell us. It has usually been assumed by the Church that it was the right side, but there is no canonical evidence for this. There are major debates by modern medical commentators as to whether the lance pierced Jesus' heart – and it has been pointed out that if this was the intention, then one might more normally have thought about piercing the left side to reach the heart. Raymond Brown, however, observes that Roman soldiers were trained to plunge in from the right and still reach the heart, because soldiers generally carried their shields on the left, knowing that the left gave easier access to the heart.[5]

One early tradition did suggest that it was the right side of Jesus which was pierced, so this may lie behind the frequent depiction of that scenario in religious art. Wherever you are reading this, I hope you will be able to go to look at a stained-glass window in a church, or a painting of this event, such as may be found in London's National Gallery. Often the artists or painters compress within their frame as much imagery as they can employ to help us understand the meaning of this event. Why not take a group from your community so that you can discuss what you see and help each other understand it? You may also like to look at a CD-ROM called *Images of Salvation, the Story of the Bible through Medieval Art*, which has a number of such pictures available for study at home.[6]

What then happened, a flow of blood and water from the side of Jesus, seemed to the disciple observers to be miraculous and, in the light of later reflection, to have sufficient significance to be made part of the Gospel narrative. It is accordingly written into the record and the eyewitness testimony emphasized.

There has been a great deal of medical discussion about this piercing and the flow of blood and water. The lance might have reached the heart, or pierced the stomach or other organs. What actually happened physiologically is uncertain, although there are a number of possible medical explanations. Usually a dead body does not bleed because the heart is no longer pumping and there is therefore no blood flow. But some medical evidence suggests that in the time immediately after death it is possible that blood could have come from the heart itself, before the blood congealed. Another possibility is that there had been internal bleeding into another cavity following the scourging, and that this was released through the wound in Jesus' side. We do not know the extent of the internal injuries inflicted by the flogging. Alternatively, a haemorrhage into the pericardial sac might have resulted in a separation of serum from the blood which was beginning to clot, which might appear as "water" and blood once it was released. Commentators who refer to the possible causes of this unexpected flow from the body of Jesus are unanimous in thinking that the Gospel writer did not mean to provoke a lengthy medical consideration, but rather to help us understand the significance of Jesus' death. The event is included for theological rather than biological purposes.[7]

There are a number of ways of understanding the theological significance of this event. First, it was imperative that the Church could be sure that Jesus had really died. There have been a few who have claimed that Jesus never really died, and that all the resurrection narratives are really recovery narratives. But that has very little foundation, since in both John's and Mark's Gospels there are requests that the death should be certified. Only if Jesus had really died was it possible for the resurrection to happen, and since Paul and others were convinced that the gospel was not worth preaching unless Jesus had risen from the dead, this piercing was an important part of the evidence. Any later claims that Jesus was so divine that he was not really human, but only appeared to be so, were also refuted by the reality of his death. Phantoms have no body and therefore cannot suffer death. This is another piece of evidence to support the contention that Jesus is really human, just like every other human being in his capacity to suffer and die.

Secondly, we read this event in the light of the whole of John's Gospel, which is emphatic in the narrative of the feeding of the 5,000 that only those who eat the flesh of the Son of Man and drink his blood are able to have eternal life. "How can that happen?" was the obvious question addressed to the larger-than-life preacher who delivered such radical teaching. This event answers that question. In his death, his body has been broken and his blood has been shed and so made available for all. For this reason, you will sometimes see pictures of the crucifixion where the artist has depicted Jesus' blood being caught in a chalice. It is a way of expressing that this blood is available to us through the sacrament of the Holy Communion, when the bread and wine are "trans-signified" so that we may eat and drink by faith.[8]

Thirdly, John's Gospel makes it clear that Jesus was killed at the same time as the Passover lambs were being prepared for the festival. In this way, the piercing echoes the Old Testament symbolism of the Passover, when the enslaved people were commanded to slay a lamb whose blood was to be daubed on the doorposts and lintels so that the angel of death would pass over them, only harming their Egyptian enemies (Exodus 12:7, 13). This piercing deepens the parallels between the Passover lambs and Jesus' death, so that we will need to understand sacrificial imagery to understand the death of Jesus. Here, the Gospel writer seems to say, the death of Jesus offers protection for the vulnerable, just as the Passover lamb was God's protection for his people in the face of slavery.

Fourthly, the flow of water encourages us to understand that the cleansing water of baptism comes from the cross, since we are forgiven on account of the death of Jesus, and as we repent and believe at our baptism we can be assured that "the blood of Jesus . . . cleanses us from all sin" (1 John 1:7–9).

His life – teaching and crucifixion

So how did the teaching of Jesus prepare him to suffer the piercing of his side? There were two key features of his life as teacher which were making him live with the anticipated end. First, there was the fact that he was teaching the disciples about the kingdom of God and about his own part in it every day of his ministry. When you teach, as I discovered myself early in my teaching career, you learn what you are teaching very well yourself. After a few years, you have no need of notes; it is written in your memory, or in your heart. If you have any integrity, then you not only have a good intellectual grasp of the subject matter, but you also find your whole life transformed by what you are teaching. For Jesus it could be no different. If he was teaching about the kingdom of God being more valuable than everything else, like a pearl of great price or a treasure hidden in a field, for both of which people sacrifice everything (Matthew 13:44–46), then he was reinforcing the message to himself that it would cost him everything too. If he was teaching about the bad tenants who were defaulting on their rent, and the owner sent his son, who was killed by the crooks because they thought they could inherit the land (Mark 12:1–12), then he was being faced with his own forthcoming destiny in Jerusalem. If he was teaching about the seasons of fasting, then he would be bound to realize that there would be a time when he, the bridegroom, would no longer be with them, and he would ponder the manner in which he was to leave them (Mark 2:18–20). We might be right to think that there was no day in which his own teaching did not mean that he was exploring in many different pictures and metaphors what his coming death meant for him and for his listeners.

Secondly, there were also, in the latter part of his ministry, the overt predictions of his death. By then, parables and images were not sufficient; the disciples needed to be forewarned of the events which were to overtake them. And so, in blunt and graphic words, Jesus began to tell them of the reality with which he had lived so closely during the previous years. As well as the implicit teaching we have already considered, there were explicit predictions of his passion. Scholars vary in their assessment of these. Some think that the details which they contain are so close to what actually happened that they must be the construction of the Church after the crucifixion and resurrection, written back into the mouth of Jesus. Others think that they may have formed part of a very early oral outline of the passion, which Mark and the other Gospel writers may have known and incorporated into their lengthier accounts, blending it with other information they had to hand. While these debates continue and may never be settled, we need to recognize that all the Gospel writers portray Jesus trying to prepare his disciples for his forthcoming death, and that none of them portray Jesus as in any way surprised by the last week of his life. He struggles with what is to come, both because he loves those who crucify him and because his suffering is in no way a pleasure to him, but he is not stunned by what happens. These things, amongst others, suggest to me that he had indeed perceived what would take place.

Jesus made every attempt to explain it all to those nearest to him, as Mark for one records. We have already noted that one such statement caused Peter to rebuke him: "Then he began to teach them that the Son of Man must undergo great suffering, and be rejected by the elders, the chief priests, and the scribes, and be killed, and after three days rise again" (Mark 8:31). Later we are told that when Jesus spoke like this, the disciples did not understand him, but were not bold enough to ask for elaboration (Mark 9:31–32). Both suffering and resurrection were foreshadowed in these sayings, which were no doubt remembered and pondered after the events as the Eleven tried to make sense of what they had witnessed. So Jesus had an increasing burden on him of attempting to help the disciples see what was approaching. And they did learn from him the sense of foreboding: "They were on the road, going up to Jerusalem, and Jesus was walking ahead of them; they were amazed, and those who followed were afraid" (Mark 10:32).

So, taking up his cross daily in his teaching ministry, Jesus was naming to himself and others the suffering towards which he was journeying. And then there were the reactions to his teaching – whether it was in public or in private. These also prepared him for future piercing. Jesus' life was not full of congenial and sympathetic companions.

We read that those who heard Jesus teach were astonished (Mark 1:22) because he taught with authority and not as the scribes, who, although they were the leading teachers of the day, were prone to refer to other authorities for their support. Despite the amazement, Jesus' teaching was not universally understood or accepted. Those whom he drew alongside him were prone to misunderstand, as were the crowds who nonetheless heard him gladly. Some were trying hard to understand, but others were attempting to trick him. The questions of those who heard him probed his meaning and purposes as sternly as the spear which later pierced his side.

Those alongside were prone to misunderstand

It is clear that, although the Twelve were privileged to hear not only the public teaching but some supplementary explanations, it was nevertheless the case that they did not always grasp Jesus' meaning at the time (see, for instance, Mark 4:11–12; 8:14–21). This is a recurring theme in the Gospels. James and John (or their mother) did not understand the nature of the kingdom, and wanted seats of honour next to Jesus (Mark 10:35–40; cf. Matthew 20:20–28). Thomas was not clear where Jesus was going when he talked in the last days of his time with them about leaving (John 14:5). Philip still did not understand at that late hour that he had been shown the Father (John 14:8). James and John wanted to command fire from heaven to fall on an unwelcoming Samaritan village, and had to be rebuked (Luke 9:55).

While it is certainly true that the teaching of Jesus was hard to comprehend, we need to recognize that the disciples were being asked to think continually outside their usual frames of reference. If we find some of the teaching of Jesus easier to understand, it is because we have benefited from decades of Church teaching which has been built on centuries of reflection. Even so, it is still the case that we do not find some parts of it easy to comprehend or to put into practice. For Jesus, there could be no easy assumption that those who were part of his new community of the kingdom would immediately understand the priorities or purposes of God.

Those alongside were always questioning him

Recognizing that they did not understand, there were occasions when the disciples themselves did question what was meant, and how these things could be. For instance, Jesus' teaching about ritual cleansing and its relationship to the commandment to honour parents and the tradition of dedicating things to God is amplified by him in private to the puzzled disciples (Mark 7:17–23). Similarly, they want to know why they failed in their attempts to help a child who was possessed, so after Jesus has dealt with the spirit and healed the boy, they ask directly about this (Mark 9:28). Many questions were put by those genuinely wanting to understand, such as the puzzle about whether those who were not followers of Jesus should be ministering in the name of Jesus (Mark 9:38–41). There is a sense in which those who were nearest to Jesus were always watching, pondering, questioning and attempting to comprehend.

Those alongside were looking for an opportunity to trip him up

Nonetheless, not all of those who came alongside Jesus had such openness to his purposes or such a desire to understand him. Some felt that they had seen and heard enough to know that there were dangerous teachings here, so their questioning was much more hostile and had a double intention. In the last week of Jesus' life, for instance, a series of trick questions was designed to force him into saying something unwise. He was asked whether it was right to pay taxes to Caesar or not. "No" would offend the occupying power and deliver him into the hands of the Romans as a stirrer of insurrection. "Yes" would deliver him into the hands of the religious leaders of his own people, who were rightly offended by the image on Roman coins of Caesar, who was claimed to be divine (Mark 12:13–17). Then there was the question about the woman who had had seven husbands, and whose wife she would be at the resurrection (Mark 12:18–27). On each occasion, Jesus refused to accept the terms in which the question was asked, and reformulated it before he offered a completely new way of approaching it. His replies demonstrate that he was entirely alert to the real purposes of those queries.

Sometimes the allegations were even more sinister – for instance that he used the power of Beelzebub rather than the power of God to heal the sick (Mark 3:22–30). All the time there were those who came alongside him with evil intent, and who did not want to learn from his teaching.

One of those alongside was becoming increasingly disillusioned

Judas was chosen from the beginning with the other Eleven. For reasons which we can only guess, however, he decided that he would offer to the authorities to reveal where Jesus might be found in a secluded place at the end of the day, so that they could arrest him without causing a popular uprising. We see from the Last Supper narrative that Jesus was acutely aware of what was happening, but kept Judas with the others to the end (Matthew 26:20–25). Alongside him throughout his ministry was one whose whole attention was on probing and judging him; who in the end was either disillusioned with the way that Jesus was proposing to establish the kingdom, or eager to precipitate the action of rebellion and thought that this was a way to do it. Whatever the reason, Jesus had learned to live with this man who was his familiar friend, but who was living alongside him only in order to give him over to piercing.

What does this mean for us as a faith community?

For his contemporaries, being alongside Jesus meant learning from him and probably from one another. This feature of life in the kingdom was so prominent that Jesus' followers were called disciples, or "learners". The Christian Church has remained a learning community ever since, although there have been peaks and troughs in its emphasis on this for every disciple. If we are to follow Jesus faithfully, then we need to recognize that we must be lifelong learners of him.

Learning alongside

I learned from an overseas bishop who was visiting the college where I teach that, in his part of the world, ministry is learned "on the job". An experienced pastor takes a trainee minister everywhere with him. This means that the trainee is there when there are mundane jobs to be done; he is there when the pastor is called to the bedside of a dying person, and sees how the pastor ministers God's grace in that circumstance. The trainee is there when the pastor prepares to lead worship, and there during the worship itself. He is there when the pastor chairs a meeting, or leads a delegation to speak to the elected political representative about local issues which are detrimental to the poor. He is there when the pastor is called upon to conduct a house cleansing or exorcism. Those trainees see not only how each thing is done, but also the manner of life led by the experienced ministers which enables them to be ready for anything.

This is how Jesus trained his disciples, and it is how many of us learn best. We watch while something is done, we try it ourselves while we have an experienced person beside us, and then we are ready to "go it alone". I have learned a great deal myself in this way. It began for me when I went to university and I was part of a group of students who had different prayer partners each week in the college where I was living. I learned how to pray from those many women who were kind enough to pray with me. They prayed in ways which I came to recognize were more Christian than my own feeble efforts. When I was a young trainee teacher, we were required to spend three weeks observing in two or three schools. I learned in those weeks both things that did work and things that did not. I can still remember some of those lessons. When I began to train as a Reader, I found that I had already learned much by watching others take services. Years of worshipping while others led had given me a good basis on which to build.

When I moved to St John's, I discovered that I had to offer spiritual counsel and pastoral support to students, for which I had no training at all. Fortunately there were both formal and informal ways of training on the job. One of the best of these was the chance to sit quietly and pray while a colleague conducted pastoral work. Later on there were chances to see how another colleague ministered to people who needed spiritual counsel or deliverance.

Those who train for ordained ministry often do placements where they have similar opportunities to learn – accompanying experienced ministers in the same kind of way as I have described above. In most churches, however, the lay people are missing many golden opportunities to learn from one another. A wise person said to me a few years ago that when he sees someone who evidently has a particular gifting from the Lord, he always asks that person to pray for him that he might learn to exercise that gift too.

Learning from one another

I often encounter a mixture of responses when I talk to people about learning from one another. Many will not venture to do something because they do not know how. Others know how to do things, but do not always want to share their wisdom with others. Sometimes that is because they do not want others to compete with them in the roles they have adopted. At other times it is because they do not have enough courage to allow someone to watch and learn from them. Or perhaps they are afraid that someone will ask them a question about why they do it this way, and they are not sure that they can answer.

During Lent it would be a good idea to identify which people in your Christian community have the gifts and skills you admire most. You might also think about which things you most want to learn to do. Then you need to pray that the people you approach will respond positively to your request to learn from them. I remember many years ago a lay person saying to a partners in mission visitor, "The clergy are always telling us to pray, but they never show us how to do it!"

It may be that praying is the skill which you most want to learn, or reading the Bible, or knowing how to visit the sick, or teaching children about Jesus, or helping with a community group. Such lessons may be available to be learned from those who already live alongside you, but whose experience is at present closed off from you.

Maybe this is the time for your church to acknowledge that it has many gifts and skills, and to declare "open season" for everyone to ask one another for help. We might want to say to someone we know, "Teach us to pray like you do," or, "Please take me with you when you visit the sick," or, "Please help – when we are in meetings, you always seem to be able to say what you think and I sit there not knowing how to start." You may be able to think of many other things which could be learned from one another.

Why should we attend to this? There are two reasons. First, discipleship is about continual learning and growth in the faith. If you have not learned anything for the last two years or so, then your discipleship is stagnating and so is your church. God has called us on a pilgrimage during which he equips us to take on more and more significant work for him. During this week, look back over the last two years and acknowledge the things which God has been teaching you, and the ways in which you have been able to use them, and thank him for the chance to serve. Alternatively, you may need to look back and see that you have not learned anything and that you have not therefore been increasing your service. In this case, a short time of repentance would be appropriate. The exceptions to that would be those who have had a period of illness or for whom age is making life an increasing struggle. But even in those circumstances you might find that God has taught you. If you have been ill, perhaps you have learned how to suffer and still bring hope to others. Or if you are becoming housebound, maybe you have been able to pray for others. I treasure the fact that two of the people who pray for me every day are elderly and not very mobile. Nonetheless, their generous faithfulness makes my ministry possible.

Secondly, many of Jesus' parables make clear that the kingdom of God *grows*. This means that we need to be learning all the time, since we need more and more people who are equipped to promote and support that growth. One of the things which is very evident to anyone who has been to a third-world country is that the majority of Christians in that context are ready to share their testimony to the love of God freely and naturally with anyone they meet. This is not because it is easier in those cultures than it is in the UK or USA. It is because Christians there have learned how to speak of their faith because every Christian they have ever met does it regularly.

What does this mean for us personally?

In the New Testament there are two relationships which the Christian is depicted as having with Jesus Christ: the first is that we are incorporated into him, and the second is that he comes to dwell in us. Paul writes, "So if anyone is *in Christ*, there is a new creation" (2 Corinthians 5:17, my italics). Elsewhere he sums up the mystery which has been made known to the Gentiles, which is "*Christ in you*, the hope of glory" (Colossians 1:27, my italics).

These two ways of understanding our relationship to Jesus Christ have been echoed down the years in many prayers. Some pray that we may be surrounded by Christ, that we may dwell in him, and others pray that he may dwell in us. Perhaps by now you have noticed that I have been using one of the prayers which asks for Christ to surround us, for us to be in him, as I have explored the issues raised in each chapter. This prayer comes in a verse from St Patrick's Breastplate. In fact, there are both kinds of prayer in this verse. Here is the whole of it.

> Christ be with me, Christ within me,
> Christ behind me, Christ before me,
> Christ beside me, Christ to win me,
> Christ to comfort and restore me,
> Christ beneath me, Christ above me,
> Christ in quiet, Christ in danger,
> Christ in hearts of all that love me,
> Christ in mouth of friend and stranger.[9]

I wrote briefly about what it means to have Christ behind us in the first chapter, about the back of Jesus. In thinking about his feet, we considered what it meant to have him before and below us, as the sure ground on which we stand and the direction in which we go. In receiving healing from his hands, we thought a little about Christ within us, reshaping and renewing us. In this section we focus on the idea of "Christ beside me, Christ to win me".

Intimacy with Jesus himself

A major purpose of incarnation was to enable human beings to be able to see, touch and hear God more clearly. Although we live in the period after the historical Jesus has departed from us, we are not in the same distanced position as those who lived before him. Through the preaching of the gospel, through the New Testament documents themselves, and through the perpetual invitation to pray, we have the opportunity to be close to Jesus in a similar way to the early disciples. The "beloved disciple" is never named in the fourth Gospel, perhaps so that each reader can see herself or himself in the stories.

The narrative of the supper at which Jesus washed feet goes on to say that Jesus predicted his betrayal to the puzzlement of the disciples. The one whom Jesus loved was reclining close to Jesus at the meal, so in response to Peter's suggestion, he asked Jesus of whom he was speaking, and was given a sign which answered the question. I think that we can see in this little exchange an invitation to continue to ask the questions of Jesus which his disciples asked throughout his life, and were asking even at this late stage. To the one who promised that he would be with us always, even to the end of the age, we can turn in disappointment, perplexity, joy and elation (Matthew 28:20). The fact that Jesus is beside us transforms our daily living, since he is there, as St Patrick suggested, to win us to himself by the love that is made evident in his wounded side.

Intimacy – ourselves with Jesus

However little the disciples understood Jesus, they found that they themselves were fully understood by him, in their weaknesses and in their potential. The same narrative shows that Jesus had understood Judas's purpose and plans, and that he made one last attempt to call him back to himself in giving him the sop, the bread which was given to an esteemed person at Passover. Jesus had also understood Peter's susceptibility to claiming more than he could deliver, and he recognized that some of the other disciples would flee. Such insight had been the case right from the beginning, when he had seen that Nathaniel was under the fig tree, and that he was without guile (John 1:47–51). Such intimacy is both immensely affirming and immensely threatening. We find it highly desirable – at last, someone who *understands* me completely! – but also highly unnerving – someone who understands me *completely*! Such knowledge explains why we sometimes feel repelled from spending time in prayer, since even the bad things cannot be hidden and we are not always strong enough to face up to them alone in the presence of God.

Living outside the constraints of our social setting

Living outside the constraints of our social setting will take us into intimacy with people who are also beside Jesus, and whose backgrounds and ways of discipleship may be deeply disturbing to us. As a young person, I found one member of my youth group very difficult to deal with, and I mentioned it to the Christian who led the group. I was probably bluntly disparaging. The leader listened carefully, then said simply, "Of such is the kingdom of God!" And that was the end of the matter. That brief exchange reshaped all my understanding of relationships. At a funeral recently, I was immensely encouraged to hear of a person who had been much helped and mentored by the fine Christian who had died. The dead man had been extremely well connected and had held down a very lucrative job; his friend was exactly the opposite, and yet they were indeed friends in the fellowship of Christ. Family and social connections had not been allowed to keep them apart.

We may want to ask ourselves whether our being alongside Jesus has taken us into any unexpected friendships, or whether we are still chiefly located in the relationships given to us by family, work and social setting. Are we willing to allow friendship with Jesus to redefine those settings for us, in the same way that they were redefined for the first disciples? That may mean working with marginal people, or it may mean not being in any way discomfited by people whom the world regards as rich or important. Who is outside your constraints, of course, will depend on where you begin. You may have met someone who has that skill of treating everyone with courtesy and respect because they are a fellow human being and not because of their position in society. I was fortunate enough to see that kind of example in one of the Christian members of my own family when I was a child. It is easy to emulate when you have a living example to study. Perhaps you could look out for such a person, if you do not think you have yet met one. His or her example may help you to be alongside Jesus and all those he gathers into the kingdom of God.

Being incorporated into Jesus Christ

A number of hymns use the image of the pierced side of Jesus as they offer prayers for us to be included in him and thereby to find safety. Here is one example.

Rock of Ages, cleft for me,
Let me hide myself in Thee;
Let the water and the blood,
From Thy riven side which flowed,
Be of sin the double cure,
Cleanse me from its guilt and power.[10]

Using the imagery of Exodus 33:21–23, the writer is praying for protection in the first two lines, and then for the cleansing which he believes is available from the shed blood and water from the side of Jesus. He acknowledges that he needs not only forgiveness for the guilt of past sins, but also release from the power of sin in his life, so he prays for a "double cure", using the healing imagery we considered in the last chapter. This hymn is close to the following Latin prayer.

Anima Christi sanctifica me.
Corpus Christi salva me.
Sanguis Christi inebria me.
Aqua lateris Christi lava me.
Passio Christi conforta me.
O bone Jesu exaudi me
In tua vulnera absconde me
Ne permittas me separari a te.
Ab Hoste maligno defende me.
In hora mortis meae voca me.
Et jube me venire a te,
Ut cum sanctis tuis laudem te.
In saecula saeculorum. Amen.

A customary English version prays in a similar way.

Soul of Christ, sanctify me.
Body of Christ, save me.
Blood of Christ, inebriate me.

> Water from the side of Christ, wash me.
> Passion of Christ, strengthen me.
> O good Jesus, hear me;
> Within thy wounds hide me;
> Suffer me not to be separated from thee;
> From the malignant enemy defend me;
> In the hour of my death call me,
> And bid me come to thee,
> That with thy saints I may praise thee
> Forever and ever. Amen.[11]

Through all these prayers runs the twin conviction that there is eternal protection from any harmful foes for those incorporated in Jesus, and that there is cleansing and strengthening in being alongside him. How such mystical union with our Saviour is to be understood is a matter for continued reflection.

Intimacy and abiding

Such an outlook links closely with Jesus' command to abide in him, which John's Gospel records for us (15:4). Whether the imagery is of Christ in us, or of us being incorporated in him, the aim is to remain in close and living connection throughout our lives. Working out how to obey that command is an important part of discipleship, but using Lent as an opportunity to reflect on these things must certainly be part of it.

Conclusion

Sacrifice and covenant

The key to understanding all the other images concerning the significance of Jesus' death is sacrifice. Without this understanding, it is impossible to pull all the other threads together. There are two reasons why people sometimes avoid using this language: they think that people in the West will not understand it, and they know that there are a huge number of different sacrifices in the Old Testament, so to speak of the death of Jesus as a sacrifice is not to convey a single idea. Nevertheless, we are going to look at this as a way of making sense of the riven side of Jesus.

It is my conviction that we must use the idea of sacrifice in referring to the death of Jesus because it is language which he himself used at the Last Supper. There he said, "This is my blood of the covenant, which is poured out for many" (Mark 14:24). This claim, in slightly different words, is made in all the accounts of the Supper (Matthew 26:28; Luke 22:20; 1 Corinthians 11:25), although there are some manuscripts which omit some of these words, which is why you may find those words in the margin of your Bible.[12]

When the old covenant was established, it was done with sacrifice, and the blood was splashed on the people and the altar as a sign of the binding nature of that covenant (Exodus 24:1–8). The new covenant was promised in the prophecy of Jeremiah, "I will make a new covenant with the house of Israel and the house of Judah. . ." (Jeremiah 31:31–34). Jesus announces to the disciples that he is about to inaugurate this new covenant and that it will be done by him pouring out his blood for many.

Some people argue that the death of Jesus is *like* a sacrifice, but is not a real sacrifice. I think we could see it another way. His death is the real sacrifice, and all the other sacrifices which people offered before his time were acceptable to God because they were anticipations of the real sacrifice of Jesus, the only sacrifice that will make a real difference to God's relationship with human beings, to human sin and salvation. This sacrifice is certainly unique. As the letter to the Hebrews makes clear, it is offered by one who is both priest and victim, on an unusual "altar", and it is not repeated.[13] All these points are seen as significant, since this sacrifice is the one to end all others. Once the new covenant is set up, there will be no need for any other living thing to be wounded and offered in this way. It will be sufficient for people to trust that this sacrifice has established a new covenant relationship with God for ever.

Sacrifice and sin forgiven

Many Old Testament sacrifices were to deal with sin. We need to consider this briefly, since this too is a way of understanding the death of Jesus that goes back to the Last Supper. Jesus said, "This is my blood of the covenant, which is poured out for many for the forgiveness of sins" (Matthew 26:28). In Leviticus, a complex set of regulations concerning repentance prescribe how sin offerings were to be made by a priest on behalf of the people, in which the blood from animal sacrifices was used to purge sin. Sacrifices for sin seem to have been regarded as in some sense polluted, so although the priests sometimes ate the meat from other sacrifices, this practice was strictly forbidden in the case of sacrifices for sin (Leviticus 6:30). Perhaps this was what was behind the phrase that Christ was made sin for us (2 Corinthians 5:21). He was the one "whom God put forward as a sacrifice of atonement by his blood, effective through faith" (Romans 3:25). There is a great debate as to whether "atonement" here means by expiation – that is, by covering sin, or by propitiation – that is, by satisfying the wrath of the person wronged, in this case God. Whichever translation is chosen (and I am inclined to think that the latter is what is meant), human sin is forgiven as people trust in Jesus' death and resurrection. Paul suggests in Ephesians 5:3 that "Christ's sacrifice of love was supremely pleasing to God", like "a fragrant offering".[14]

Sacrifice and Passover

We have already explored some of what this might mean, and it is undoubtedly part of the backcloth against which the early Church began to understand why Jesus died. Paul, for instance, writes, "For our paschal lamb, Christ, has been sacrificed" (1 Corinthians 5:7), and we are invited to celebrate the freedom which he has won for us. It is interesting that Luke records that at the transfiguration, Moses and Elijah were talking to Jesus about his "departure", or exodus, "which he was about to accomplish at Jerusalem" (Luke 9:30–31). Although Luke is less forthcoming about sacrificial imagery to explain the significance of Jesus' death, he seems to be saying that Jesus was prepared for this sacrificial death by the revelation imparted to him by the law and the prophets, in the persons who appeared to him. The exodus theme inevitably held within it the necessity of paschal lambs being slain. Without the shedding of blood, there would be no exodus.

The sacrifice of Jesus was unique. It could not be contained in any one Old Testament category. The three different kinds of sacrifice which we have considered briefly here were all influential in helping Christians come to understand what God had done in Jesus' death, by his pierced side and shed blood.

QUESTIONS AND IDEAS

In a group

1 Do a social analysis of the church where you worship. To what extent is it as inclusive as we have seen the disciples of Jesus to be? If it is extremely wide in its membership, what do you think has encouraged that to happen? If it is not embracing many different kinds of people, what might you do to encourage that to happen?

2 Ask one of the group to read John 19:31–37 slowly and with good pauses so that everyone can enter into the story imaginatively. Allow a good space of time at the end, before asking people whether there is anything that they want to share with the group.

3 Consider whether you agree that Jesus' own teaching was preparing him for his death.

4 Does your Christian community encourage people to learn from one another? If so, share with the group what you have learned by this method. If not, are there things which you could do in the group to begin the process of sharing with one another the things you have learned as Christians? You may need to begin by talking to one another about what you most want to learn.

By yourself

1 How widely inclusive is your group of Christian friends?

2 Read John 19:31–37 slowly and with good pauses so that you can enter into the story imaginatively. Allow a good space of time at the end, to consider where you find yourself in the story, and what you feel about being there. You may wish to write a prayer which expresses what you feel.

3 Do you find it easier to think of yourself as hidden in Christ, or as Christ in you? Which of the prayers would you find it easiest to pray? Can you pray both of them?

4 Recall the last occasion when you were able to spend time alongside Jesus, so that you could voice your questions to him and allow him to speak to you about all that he can see in you. Is this a regular feature of your devotions? If not, ask God to show you how you can enter into this close "abiding in Jesus".

Something to pray about

[Based on Jesus' invitation to take his yoke upon us in Matthew 11.29]

Yoke me to you, Lord Jesus Christ, that I may stay close beside you all the days of my life;
Yoke me to you, dear Lord, so that I may abide in you, and you in me.
Yoke me to you, Lord Jesus Christ, that I may learn of you, and become more like you,

Yoke me to you, dear Lord, so that I may teach others your
  ways.
Yoke me to your people, Lord Jesus Christ, so that I may
  embrace all those you have embraced;
Yoke me to them, dear Lord, that we may be one.
Yoke me to you, Lord Jesus Christ, for you are gentle and
  humble of heart,
Yoke me to you, dear Lord, so I may find rest for my soul.
Amen.

FOR FURTHER READING

J. Bishop, *The Day Christ Died*, London: Weidenfeld and
  Nicholson, 1957.

Raymond Brown, *The Death of the Messiah*, New York:
  Doubleday, 1994.

A. Heron, *Table and Tradition*, Edinburgh: Handsel Press,
  1983.

A. Lincoln, *Ephesians*, Word Biblical Commentary, Dallas:
  Word, 1990.

HIS HEAD
SPIRIT-ANOINTING AND CRUCIFIXION

His body

We do not know what Jesus looked like, so as you read this chapter each of you will have a different image of his head, face or profile. Perhaps you may think of a classic depiction of Jesus such as one sees in sculpture or art. Maybe you recall an artisan you have met whose strong head and neck muscles help you to imagine the appearance of Jesus. However we imagine him, we know that soon after he began his public ministry he was recognized by many hundreds of people, who flocked to see him and to hear the words he spoke. We are surely right to think that such teaching was the overflowing of a mind set on God and the things of God throughout his early life.

The Gospels are unanimous in affirming that Jesus was well versed in the things of God, and Luke tells us that he had three days of deep conversation with the leading teachers of the time in Jerusalem, asking them questions (Luke 2:46). Some scholars have doubted whether a child from such a poor and small place as Nazareth could have learned to read and write. They note that there is no archaeological evidence of a synagogue in Nazareth in the time of Jesus,[1] and they conclude that there might have been no scrolls either, which makes it unlikely that any inhabitants would have learned to read. However, people could come together in a number of different ways, in houses or the open air, and Luke is certainly clear in speaking of the synagogue in Nazareth as though it is a public building (4:1–29), so it may be best to follow this hint, despite the lack of evidence on the ground. And even if Nazareth did lack learned people, then it was near to Sepphoris, which was certainly big enough to have such expertise.

The picture which the Gospels present is one of Jesus not only knowing the Scriptures but also being "filled with wisdom" and "increasing in wisdom" (Luke 2:40, 52), so that in adult life his teaching became famous and has endured for twenty centuries. We may imagine him walking the hills and feasting his eyes on the natural world which fill his parables, drinking in the pictures of human life which he saw and which reappear in his sayings and sermons. His eyes were very attuned to detail – did he not notice a widow putting all she had into the collection? Likewise, his ears heard the tone of people's voices so that he knew when to challenge and when to encourage, and could even perceive the thoughts of their hearts. His mind was accustomed to reflection long before he began his public ministry. The wisdom of God with which he was filled and in which he increased shone out in his everyday dealings with people as he avoided traps, ministered to people's hearts and saw to the root of their problems with unerring accuracy. Jesus learned as a child to open his mouth so that God could fill it with wisdom.

His wounds

There are a number of different ways in which the head of Jesus was wounded, although they are not always counted as wounds. During the trials, several different actions were directed at Jesus' head: spitting, blindfolding or covering, striking or slapping, and crowning with thorns. The Gospels do not give us identical descriptions, so our discussion will need to be a composite of what they say. In broad terms, there were two sets of abuse in connection with the two sets of "trials" recorded in the New Testament – the trial before the Jewish authorities, and the trials before the Roman authorities. All four Gospels refer to both sets of mockeries. At the end of the Jewish trial, Jesus is subject to taunts which are chiefly connected to his prophetic role. At the Roman trial, he is subject to taunts which are chiefly connected to his kingly role. In all the Gospels the mockeries which are chiefly to do with his priestly role, namely his willing self-sacrifice in offering his life for others, are hurled at him while he is on the cross, but these final mockeries are restricted to verbal abuse.

The kiss of Judas

I think we must regard the kiss of Judas as the first occasion when Jesus' head was wounded. The reasons why Judas betrayed Jesus are shrouded in mystery in the Gospels. It may have been for financial gain, or because Jesus was not behaving as Judas expected a Messiah to behave, or he may have intended to precipitate Jesus into some kind of miraculous saving act for the people. Theories abound, but for whatever human reasons, Judas agreed with the religious leaders that he would lead them to Jesus at a time when there would be no crowds to protest against the arrest. Judas knew, however, that he was unlikely to find Jesus without some of his fellow disciples being present, so there was a potential problem in apprehending the right man. Some kind of sign had to be arranged, and it was agreed that this should be in the manner of greeting. In contemporary terms, we could imagine someone saying, "I'll greet them all with a brief word, but the one I shake hands with is the one you want!"

In Greek and Roman society, people did not exchange kisses in public places, because it was a family greeting reserved for the home.[2] In Jewish society it seems to have been part of the expectation for house guests, since Jesus rebuked Simon the Pharisee for not offering him this courtesy at his dinner party (Luke 7:45). Perhaps it was customary for the disciples to greet Jesus in this way, as some disciples of other rabbis at that time seem to have done. Such a kiss could be on the hand or foot; if it was on the head it was cheek to cheek, never mouth to mouth.[3] If that was the custom between Jesus and the disciples, then it is easy to understand why early followers of Jesus continued this practice with one another, greeting fellow Christians with a kiss (Romans 16:16; 1 Peter 5:14). To rabbis of the time, it was simply a sign of respect, so Judas's kiss would not have made the others suspicious when it happened. That kiss has become notorious, however, because a sign of affection and honour was given with completely opposite intentions, as a mark of identity for execution. Such duplicity scorned the friendship which Jesus offered his disciples. It was a betrayal which sentenced Jesus to capture by his enemies, and Judas must have realized that it was highly likely to lead to a most violent death.

It is for this reason that this brief salutation has been taken as the first assault on the person of Jesus. It was not physically painful compared with what was yet to come, but it was personally destructive, violating a special bond of trust and using a sign of friendship to transform the relationship, on Judas's side, into vicious enmity (Mark 14:44b–45).

Jesus embraced the passion into which he was then launched: "Friend, do what you are here to do" (Matthew 26:50). Even the question which Jesus posed in Luke's Gospel, "Judas, is it with a kiss that you are betraying the Son of Man?" (22:48), does not attempt to turn aside the arrest which will lead to devastating physical suffering.

The spitting

There are two occasions on which spitting is described. First, immediately after the trial before the high priest, "Some began to spit on him, to blindfold him, and to strike him, saying to him, 'Prophesy!'" (Mark 14:65). This spitting is almost certainly contemptuous, because Jesus has been judged to be a blasphemer for his reply to the question about his identity. "Again the high priest asked him, 'Are you the Messiah, the Son of the Blessed One?' Jesus said, 'I am; and "you will see the Son of Man seated at the right hand of the Power", and "coming with the clouds of heaven"'" (Mark 14:61–62). This disdainful spitting may have been the prescribed response to a person found guilty of blasphemy, since it seems to be an ancient rebuke (Numbers 12:14; cf. Deuteronomy 25:9). We can only imagine what it meant for the Son of the Blessed One first to see people coming up and spitting in his face, and then to be blindfolded so that he could not identify the spitters visually, as the offence became part of another kind of taunting. We remember that he could not remove himself from their foul breath, nor lift his arm to wipe away their spittle. Physically, he bears their iniquities (Isaiah 53:4–5).

Secondly, there was sneering and spitting on Jesus while he was in the power of Pilate. In "the courtyard of the palace (that is, the governor's headquarters) . . . they called together the whole cohort. And they clothed him in a purple cloak;

and after twisting some thorns into a crown, they put it on him. And they began saluting him, 'Hail, King of the Jews!' They struck his head with a reed, spat upon him, and knelt down in homage to him. After mocking him, they stripped him of the purple cloak and put his own clothes on him" (Mark 15:16ff.; Matthew 27:27). The way this occasion is described makes clear that this violation of Jesus is not just done by one person, but by several, maybe many. He has already been condemned to death before this second spitting attack. We cannot help but contrast the gentleness with which Jesus used his own spittle, to heal the blindness of the sufferer at Bethsaida, with the derisory acts of his enemies, who use their spittle to inflict further indignity on the one who could have healed their spiritual blindness as easily as he had healed that physical blindness outside Bethsaida (Mark 8:22–26).

The blindfolding

"Now the men who were holding Jesus began to mock him and beat him; they also blindfolded him and kept asking him, 'Prophesy! Who is it that struck you?' They kept heaping many other insults on him" (Luke 22:63–65; cf. Mark 14:65). Waiting for the first inquisition before the leaders of his own people, Jesus' sight is denied as well as his freedom. A great many pictures of the atrocities allegedly perpetrated against prisoners in Iraq suggest that the old torment of holding prisoners blindfolded so that they become disorientated remains, illegally, in vogue today. These pictures give content to something which, in the West, we may be more accustomed to thinking of in terms of a children's game. In the house of the high priest, this was anything but harmless fun. The harsh reality is that a prisoner is made very vulnerable by the covering of the eyes, because there is no knowing where the next assault will come from. In these circumstances nerves already screaming danger are heightened further by the unfamiliar sounds and smells which surround the prisoner. We rightly call this torture. The fact that in Jesus' case it was done in a religious context, in which there was an attempt to make him "prophesy" or guess who had hit him, does not diminish the appalling nature of the attack. The Gospels do not give us a clear picture of how long this degradation may have lasted.

The striking

Hitting, beating or striking someone on any part of their anatomy is bound to cause pain, but there are certain parts which are known to be particularly physically painful and other parts which are recognized as causing special offence. Slapping someone on the arm, however wrong, is not the same as slapping someone in the face. The striking of Jesus' head or face is recorded in a number of contexts, and it is not always clear why it happens, but part of the nature of evil is that there is rarely a rational explanation of why assaults happen as they do. In one case, it seems as if the intention is purely to insult Jesus as a response to his implicit claim to be the "Son of the Blessed": "Then they spat in his face and struck him; and some slapped him, saying, 'Prophesy!'" (Matthew 26:67) John's Gospel perhaps makes this even clearer: "One of the police standing nearby struck Jesus on the face, saying, 'Is that how you answer the high priest?' Jesus answered, 'If I have spoken wrongly, testify to the wrong. But if I have spoken rightly, why do you strike me?'" (18:22–23). Perhaps righteous indignation at Jesus' reply, on the part of the police, made one of them slap him, possibly on his mouth as a physical expression of outrage.

It may also have been an attempt to ascertain whether Jesus had the powers which others claimed he had, since there is some suggestion that he should identify those who struck him. In the custody of Pilate, however, there is no such ulterior motive; this is sheer violence. "And the soldiers wove a crown of thorns and put it on his head, and they dressed him in a purple robe. They kept coming up to him, saying, 'Hail, King of the Jews!' and striking him on the face" (John 19:2–3). Indeed, Matthew records that they also "took the reed and struck him on the head" (27:30). Physically the pain could not be compared to the flogging, but the intention was to humiliate and disgrace. Without realizing it, these different tormenters enabled Jesus to fulfil the prophecy of Isaiah concerning the suffering servant of the Lord: "I gave my back to those who struck me, and my cheeks to those who pulled out the beard" (50:6).

The crowning with thorns

After the trial, the soldiers were allowed to have some cruel fun at Jesus' expense before he was flogged and crucified. It is significant that his crowning is juxtaposed to his death, for he will be given the crown and authority to rule in the resurrection, which proclaims his final victory over sin, death and the devil. Not until this point has he been crowned, although throughout his ministry he has been ushering in the kingdom, and using the kingdom's power in miracles and preaching.

What we would expect for any normal king, first crowning and then exercise of power, is overturned in this unconventional moment. Even the nature of the coronation is exceptional. When it does happen, it is not the freewill offering of those who honour him, but the sport of those who will murder him. The crowning at this point says that his kingship is most clearly seen in suffering, in shedding blood and in humiliation. His kingship is characterized by utter self-giving love, rather than by force or by humiliation of others. But he is king even over those who ridicule and mock him. And the kingship which he has already been exercising, in overcoming Satan in the lives of the possessed and in establishing God's rule in people's hearts, cannot be taken away from him even at this point. The irony is that those who have fun at his expense are unwittingly making clear that he is king for ever. The death for which they prepare him guarantees this, as the gateway to resurrection.

"And the soldiers wove a crown of thorns and put it on his head, and they dressed him in a purple robe. They kept coming up to him saying, 'Hail, King of the Jews!' and striking him on the face" (John 19:2–3). A crown of leafy twigs was more usually made without the thorns, for it was often used as a wreath to be awarded to a victor in a race. Although the thorns must have pierced his flesh, perhaps penetrating below the skin of his forehead and remaining there after the crown had been removed, the suffering inflicted is simply recorded, but not emphasized, by the Gospel writers. Commentators note that it is possible to portray the crown of thorns so that it forms a shape like the rays of the sun, as normal leafy wreaths were often depicted on Roman emperors.[4] Art captures the theological significance of this cruel gesture.

The offering of sour wine

On the cross Jesus was offered sour wine, which may have been the kind of wine normally issued to the soldiers. On the first occasion, it seems to have been offered as a kind of narcotic to numb the pain, but Jesus refused to drink it (Mark 15:23). Matthew says that the wine had been mixed with gall, so was undrinkable (27:34).[5] On the second occasion, it seems to have been part of the mockery of Jesus (Luke 23:36), either because it was not the kind of wine which a king would drink, or because it was a mockery of his cry to God, which the bystanders misheard as a call to Elijah to save him. Those who offered wine may have done so to keep him alive a little longer, to see whether Elijah would come to rescue him.[6] In any case, the culmination of the affronts to the head of Jesus are these offers of wine before and during his crucifixion – offers which in no way mitigated the suffering and the humiliation.

His life – Spirit-anointing and crucifixion

What were the key ways in which the head of Jesus was prepared for the suffering which was to come? What kept him faithful when he faced such an onslaught?

First, throughout his ministry there had not been the kind of comfort which most readers of this book would take for granted – indeed, there probably never was much comfort in the simple home in which he grew up. But from the moment he began his itinerant preaching, "The Son of Man [had] nowhere to lay his head" (Luke 9:58). This does not necessarily mean that he slept rough on his teaching and healing journeys, although he may have done that sometimes. Usually he seems to have depended on those to whom he preached offering him hospitality, which we must imagine he accepted whatever the state of the home, since that is what he taught his disciples to do: "Remain in the same house, eating and drinking whatever they provide, for the labourer deserves to be paid. Do not move about from house to house. . ." (Luke 10:7).

Secondly, he had prepared himself as his vocation became increasingly clear. Thus "he set his face" to go up to Jerusalem (Luke 9:51). Despite the disciples' fear (Mark 10:32), Jesus set the pace and seems to have understood the risks.

Thirdly, one narrative above all suggests that the head of Jesus had been prepared for such a battering, and that is the story of the woman anointing his head (Mark 14:1–11). An anointing story comes in each of the Gospels, but there are such differences between this story and the anointing of Jesus' feet, which we have already considered, that I take it this one must be based on a different event and is not a second version of the same occurrence. This anointing speaks of Jesus' messiahship, his suffering, his death and resurrection. All of these are prophesied in this one narrative.

The anointing of Jesus' head

Mark begins the passion account with this story. The opponents of Jesus were seeking to arrest him by stealth, and Judas went to betray him. The verses which frame our anointing story are all about the proposed betrayal and arrest. It is one of Mark's famous "sandwiches", where dark plans of treachery and duplicity are set around an act of sheer love. Judas's greedy act of betrayal stands in stark contrast to the woman's generous and loving actions, and the drama is heightened by this juxtaposition. We see here how Jesus divides people: those who are not for him are against him. He has inspired in some the desire to kill, but in this woman he has called up a deep devotion. We may surely say that Jesus arouses passionate feelings.

Jesus was in Bethany, two miles from Jerusalem, and probably lodged there in the last week of his life. He was in the house of Simon the leper, who had probably been healed, but we do not have the story of his restoration in the Gospel narratives. Jesus and the others were reclining at table. An anonymous woman came in, carrying an alabaster jar or perfume flask, probably without handles and with a long neck, such as was usually used in funeral rites. It would have been sealed to preserve the perfume. The jar contained pure perfume or oil, or the oil of pistachio nuts which was used as the basis of perfume. Nard was an Indian plant much prized in the ancient world. The custom was to break the neck of the jar and pour the contents all over the deceased. In this case, the woman used the oil to anoint the head of Jesus. The bystanders were indignant, because the perfume was worth nearly a year's wages. Perhaps it was the woman's family heirloom. Perhaps she had spent all her own or her family's savings on it. It was a costly little bottle of perfume. No wonder the onlookers thought it was wasted! Jesus, however, sprang to the woman's defence.

In Mark the story is short of detail. We are not told that this woman was a sinner with a bad conscience, or that it was Mary or someone else. This woman is anonymous. We simply have to imagine what might have precipitated her action, for Mark wants us, his readers, to focus on the act of breaking and pouring. He offers two hints as to her motives.

First, this was an unconventional act. It was almost certainly a male-only dinner party, and during the meal she forced her attention on Jesus, driven by strong feelings. We might remember the woman with the haemorrhages, and the Syro-Phoenician woman whose daughter needed help. Like them, this woman was determined to get to Jesus. She felt compelled to anoint him, and nothing and no one was going to prevent her.

Secondly, it was a public act, not a private gift. The scent must have pervaded the whole house. If you have ever emptied a bottle of perfume in a room, you will know exactly what effect it has. Everyone present instantly knew what had happened; there was no concealing it. How could she make a public scene like that? How could she force her attention on Jesus? Karl Barth suggests that "so seriously is love self-giving that his life is an 'eccentric' life, i.e. one which has its centre outside of itself."[7] The truly loving act is not self-conscious. She did not think of herself, she thought only of Jesus. She did not think of the onlookers, she thought only of honouring him. The woman's actions sprang out of the fact that she was entirely focused on Jesus. She must have been deeply shocked when she found herself the centre of attention and the subject of reproach.

The onlookers were not unreasonable. It was customary to give to the poor at Passover, and if they were themselves poor, then they would have understood only too well what that costly little bottle might have meant to the destitute. They had it right: Jesus was always telling them to be concerned for the poor. And they had an important part to play in this story, for their rude suggestion that this had been wasted on Jesus provoked the most significant comment that Mark conveys. But they also had it wrong, because on this occasion there were other considerations which took precedence over the usual standards.

Dennis Nineham comments that "our evidence doesn't suggest that Jesus is likely to have gone in very much for perfume".[8] Whether or not this is true, Jesus could see that the woman's action was a spontaneous expression of her sense of the worship which was due to him. Jesus offered her his protection, and he commended her and accepted the gift of her love. He saw her motives, and therefore he rebuked the protesters. There is a three-point explanation for this.

First, the disciples would always have the poor, but they would not always have Jesus with them. At the very beginning of his ministry he had made that clear in a little saying about the bridegroom who would not always be with them (Mark 2:18–20). That early hint, and the more explicit passion predictions, were intended to help them understand that Jesus would not always be there. In the context of his imminent departure, this was not the time for social concern. Their protest might have been rephrased, "Isn't this expensive ointment wasted on Jesus?" Without thinking, they had offered an implicit insult to the one who had become poor for their sake. Did he not deserve their honour, their love, and perhaps even their comfort as he faced his end? The woman's action, Jesus had to explain, was a prediction of his death.

Secondly, it was also a prediction of his resurrection. She did what she could: she anointed Jesus' body beforehand. "If you want to prepare me for burial, then you'd better do it now, because I won't be dead for long," might be another way of putting it. The fact that Jesus was anointed before he died was a prophetic act which pointed forward to the third day and the resurrection.

Thirdly, it made clear the saving efficacy of those two events, which would become known worldwide. "Wherever the good news is proclaimed in the whole world, what she has done will be told in remembrance of her" (Mark 14:9). Karl Barth suggests, "What clearly emerges is that Jesus not only defends unconditionally the act of the woman but in all solemnity acknowledges that it is a good act which belongs necessarily to the history of salvation even though it seems to be wholly superfluous, an act of sheer extravagance which can serve 'only' the purpose of representing direct and perfect self-giving to him."[9]

Does it belong necessarily to the act of salvation? Do we read the story to remember her, or because she did something uniquely important for Jesus in God's plan of salvation? Not only did she love and give lavishly; not only did she alone prepare him for his death while all the rest tried to tell him he was wrong or lure him away from his destiny: she anointed the anointed one, the Messiah, for his death and in preparation for his resurrection. It was an unconventional anointing, but the embodiment of his messiahship. She made a royal anointing of his head, and this is linked with his death and resurrection, because they are at the very heart of his kingship, his messiahship. This is a passage which holds up to us an example of unconditional self-giving. It warns against misjudging the motives of others. But it is primarily a passage which presents to us Jesus the Messiah, the anointed one. He is unconventionally anointed, not by a priest or a prophet, but by an anonymous woman. She is the one who anoints the chosen one of God.

The anointing of the Spirit

In every other chapter we have been tracing the connection between the early life of Jesus and the cross. In this chapter, we trace the cross as the source of all that comes afterwards. Thinking about the head of Jesus makes us consider the way in which his anointing with oil (prefigured in his anointing with the Spirit at his baptism) and his anointing with death and new life (that is, his being submerged under its flood) enables us to be anointed with that same Spirit when we are willing for the same water baptism and the consequent anointing or submerging in death and new life. We might think of the beginning and the end of Jesus' ministry as being marked by an anointing – the first in the Spirit at water-baptism, the second in oil at death-baptism. (Jesus, you will remember, asked the pushy disciples James and John whether they could be baptized with the same baptism as himself when they tried to claim, without the suffering, the honour of seats on either side of him [Mark 10:38].)

After Jesus had been anointed with both Spirit and oil, as prophets, priests and kings were anointed in the Old Testament, all those who became part of his body, the Church, found themselves partaking in the same anointing – his anointing. Those who trust in the Son of God and participate in his life will automatically receive the Spirit as members of his body. This is the reason why the Spirit is much more widely available after the time of Jesus than before. The anointing with the Holy Spirit will inevitably draw us into the same movement of self-giving love which enabled Jesus to offer his head to the smiters, and which will enable us to die to selfishness and live with the new resurrection life which comes from him. John's Gospel links the gift of the Spirit to the death of Jesus very precisely: "For as yet there was no Spirit [or the Spirit was not yet given], because Jesus was not yet glorified" (John 7:39). The moment of his glorifying, we remember, is the moment of his death.

What does this mean for us as a faith community?

Since Jesus is the anointed king, it is appropriate to begin with his own teaching and living out of the kingdom of God when we come to consider how we might join hands with others to extend his gentle and life-transforming rule to the world, which our anointing in the Holy Spirit will necessarily involve. This anointing truly teaches us about Jesus: "As for you, the anointing that you received from him abides in you, and so you do not need anyone to teach you. But as his anointing teaches you about all things, and is true and is not a lie . . . abide in him" (1 John 2:27).

When we read about kings who lived at the time of Jesus, or about monarchs at other times when their power was not curtailed by law or democracy, we recognize that the character of the king influences the lives of those who are subjects in very significant ways. Under a good, wise king there is some hope of justice and peace; under a morally bankrupt king there will be injustice and peace will be endangered; under a capricious king there is no way to know what may happen, good or bad.

Justice and compassion

When we think of the way in which Jesus expressed his kingship, we are struck first of all by his consistency and his utter lack of capriciousness. There is a consistency between who he is and what he does that inspires people, however misguidedly, to seek to make him king (John 6). What was it about him that made them want to see him in a place of temporal authority? The Gospel writers suggest that it was his capacity to provide bread for the hungry! Their cynicism may be overplayed, although we know that a good government will take seriously the need to provide basic food for everyone – which is one of the reasons why the current government in Zimbabwe, for example, is so evil. Whether or not it might be legitimate to reassign land, it cannot be right to do so without a comprehensive plan for sustaining the agricultural programme so that all may eat.

Perhaps, however, it was the compassion Jesus showed in the miraculous feeding of the 5,000 which people considered the more attractive characteristic in the long term. And remember that they had spent a long time listening to him teaching. Such wisdom must have come from his lips that they longed not only to learn about God's kingdom but also to ask him to establish it among them. That response was surely entirely appropriate.

What might he have spoken about on that occasion? Well, if we may borrow from the other Gospels, we might be able to imagine that Jesus spoke of the way in which there would be equal blessing for all in the kingdom (the parable of a day's wages for all, see Matthew 20:1–16). Of course, he also made it clear that each person would need to be a responsible steward of the capacities God had entrusted to him or her (the parable of the talents, see Matthew 25:14–30), and that God would take seriously the laziness of any who refused that task. Perhaps it was his insistence that justice would be applied fairly which inspired them to ask him to exercise justice over them. The parable of the sheep and the goats must surely have encouraged a poor crowd who did not always receive prison visits, help in sickness, and so on (see Matthew 25:32–46). But it must have been the mercy that was to accompany this justice which most encouraged them – of which they heard in the parable of the debtors (see Matthew 18:23–35).

Obviously the nature of the kingdom as being both now and not yet had passed over the heads of this crowd in John's Gospel, but the assurance that God rules in Jesus was not lost on them and they were ready for the rule of God, which they hoped he would bring to them immediately.

Later there was also the triumphal entry into Jerusalem. On this occasion Jesus both owned and reconstructed his kingship, by his choice of a donkey instead of a war horse as his mount. Accepting the royal welcome which was accorded him as he came into the city over which he was rightful king, he rode towards the events in which his kingship would be consummated, and in which he would reign from the tree of crucifixion.

How can we exercise compassion?

So, we rightly ask, what would it look like for us to work for the kingdom of which Jesus is the rightful king?

A few months ago, I was asked to take an assembly at a local secondary school. I agreed somewhat reluctantly. It is a very long time since I taught in school, and I felt very unconnected to teenage issues. Worse news then followed: the school was following a set of themes and I was invited to speak on the subject of "charity". As I told them at the start of the assembly, I felt as though their teacher had set me an essay which I did not want to do! So I borrowed the structure of a book I read many years ago by Charles Elliott, *Comfortable Compassion*,[10] because it has been so helpful to me in my thinking about discipleship, and drew on my own experiences.

Elliott's basic thesis is that Christians need to pass through three stages in their response to the demands of the kingdom of God. The first stage, which most people find easiest, is to give generously to needy cases. In my situation, that means making sure that when people beg on the streets, I ask them if they are hungry, and if they are I fetch them some sandwiches and tea.

The second stage is for us to realize that, if we are to do anything more than simply calm our consciences and help a few people on a haphazard basis, we must organize something which will deal with the situation more effectively.

That leads us to creating charitable societies and making regular donations – to Help the Aged, for example, or a homelessness project in the city where we live.

As we work in this kind of way, however, we realize that both of these approaches are really only emergency measures for individuals or for larger groups. They both address the problem, but they do not uncover the root of the problem and try to solve it there. This leads us on to the third stage, the level of kingdom work which always requires us to get involved in politics, be that local or national, and this is the area from which many Christians shy away. And yet Christians of previous centuries have had a good track record of undertaking this ground-level work in education, health care and the slave trade, to name but a few areas of influence. In some places they have also been at the forefront of challenging the exploitation of workers and child labour, which has been the root cause of widespread poverty and ill health.

While you are considering your response, I want to suggest to you that you and your Christian community locally, your church or fellowship, might address this question at these three levels, *in your locality*. This is often where we can make a special difference – and we need to be on the lookout for the local opportunities which present themselves from time to time. One clear instance of the first level in my own experience occurred when I was a member of a church in Scunthorpe. A number of refugee families came to the area from Uganda, settled there because we had a good number of council houses available. Women from the church in which I worshipped offered to teach wives and mothers English, to help them with shopping and relating to social agencies, and to offer them basic domestic utensils. Such practical help in a local emergency, organized by the church, should be part of the life of every Christian community – and of course it often is in some of the needier parts of the world, which have a lot to teach those of us in more affluent areas.

At the second level, it might be possible to make it part of the church's stewardship to address in a more systematic fashion the ongoing needs of your locality. Another project with which I am familiar is organized twice each year at the college where I teach. It originally developed in an attempt to help a child through education, but it has been going for so long now that, while it retains the child's name – the KWON sale – the proceeds are sent to a hospital in Uganda, which depends on these finances. This is a major operation, which takes over the college for a weekend, but it could easily be done in most church premises. It helps families in this country too. On the given Friday night, large numbers of people arrive with children's clothes, toys and equipment, all neatly labelled with price and the name and address of the vendor. These are arranged on tables by kind. When the sale starts on Saturday morning, the salespeople take the money and the labels, so that when the sale has finished vendors can come back during the afternoon to receive a set proportion of the sale price – the balance being sent as a donation to the hospital in Uganda. One of these sales happens in November, prior to Christmas, and the other in the summer. Any unsold items can be claimed during a specified period and any unwanted things go to a local charity. Another church I visited in a very poor area of the country had begun asking local rummage sales if they could have any leftover clothes. They washed and mended anything they could obtain and sent lorry-loads of garments to Eastern Europe when there was major need. Imagination and creativity made it possible for people who did not think they had very much to share to organize a contribution to charitable work.

At the third level, the church needs to pray about what its particular issue might be. We cannot do everything, but that should not stop us from doing something. It might be an occasional event. Many local churches are the only locations where all the candidates in a local or national election are invited to a public meeting at which electors can ask questions about policies and proposals. This is an ideal opportunity to serve the neighbourhood and also to hold representatives accountable. This can be done ecumenically, so that the meetings are sponsored by all the churches in an area.

Moreover, in many denominations, national campaigns or protests begin at the local level. Thus, a Church of England resolution which undoubtedly rattled the company concerned was passed initially at the local level before it was taken into the national arena, protesting at the irresponsibility of advertising breast milk substitutes in the Third World, where mother's milk is always best because it is always the right strength and temperature and is hygienic. Children die from powdered milk being made up with dirty water. This is a good example of a way in which the national and international Church can bring pressure to bear on industrial and political leaders.

It is our responsibility in the West, where there are good communications and also very often the levers of power in the global village, to ensure that the concerns of Christians in the Two-Thirds World are brought to public attention so that change can happen. This may mean a long and difficult campaign – the Jubilee Campaign is a prime example. We should not underestimate the power, finances and pressures which will be massed against us if we begin to speak on behalf of the poor, but we also ought to realize that, in this age of fast communications, we cannot claim ignorance as an excuse for allowing Christians in other parts of the world to suffer, often directly, as a result of policies which we could well change if we were more politically vocal.

What does this mean for us personally?

The anointing of which I have written above is for us personally as well as for our Christian community. When we decide to accept Jesus' rule in our individual lives, it will mean being transformed by the renewing of our minds (Romans 12:2) as we come to understand what it means for us to be anointed with the same Holy Spirit as Jesus. And that, as the rest of Romans 12 makes clear, will mean living a very different kind of life from the one we had before we came to faith.

Being holy

The heart of God's intention for us is that we should be holy. It may not be easy to imagine this – it is a big task which God sets before us. Paul often writes about how we might make progress in this. In 1 Thessalonians it seems as if Paul is inviting us to recognize that God gives us the same Holy Spirit with which Jesus was anointed. Our relationship with God is to be one in which we find ourselves partnered by his Holy Spirit, as if we were dancing in exact formation like ballroom dancers. The idea of a dance with God's Holy Spirit is one way of reading this beautiful piece of dialectic theology.

God sanctifies us – this is the work of God: "For God did not call us to impurity but in holiness. Therefore whoever rejects this rejects not human authority but God, who also gives his Holy Spirit to you" (1 Thessalonians 4:7–8). Being holy becomes our work as partners with him. He will take the lead, we need to follow. He will invite us to be so close to him that he can empower us to serve and to live lives that express the kingdom of God. But we will also need to play our part. We may feel, in our Christian lives, as if our feet are not dancing the right steps, so in frustration we want to sit out the dance. Our prayer needs to be that we will become so well adapted to what God's Holy Spirit is doing in us that we never want to stop dancing at all. Growth in holiness is first God's work, but it is also our task to welcome him and to be ready for whatever that might involve.

Holiness is only going to come if we do not quench the Spirit (1 Thessalonians 5:19) and if we are ready to use our minds to think about what we are doing (1 Thessalonians 5:20–22). Sometimes, when we watch people dancing, we see what we think is an unusual dance couple, maybe because of their differing styles or their unsuitable proportions. However unusually matched, a pair who pay careful attention to one another can nevertheless be brilliant dancers. We may imagine that the partnership of the Spirit with someone who has come to faith in Jesus makes for a very "odd couple". That, of course, is true for every one of us who is filled with the Spirit of God; we are all in one sense "unsuitable partners" for him. But he delights to dance with us in the same kind of way as an adult at a ceilidh leads a child onto the floor and helps that little person to dance as part of a reel. The unevenness of the partnership should not deter us from keeping in step with the Spirit. If we are growing in holiness, it is because God has invited us to be his partner and we have accepted that offer. As we think about what that might mean for us personally, we need to note that this is often where the battle is lost: we think that we are individually so powerless that we cannot make a difference. This is not true. We have already seen that being anointed with the Spirit is like being partnered with God, who is able to lead us through the most complex dances in the cause of the kingdom. So perhaps we need to begin by allowing ourselves to hear the words which Jesus said to the first disciples as he left them to return to his Father: "All authority in heaven and on earth has been given to me. Go therefore. . ." (Matthew 28:18–19). If we feel ill-equipped to make disciples, or to serve in any other kind of way, we also need to hear the one whose authority was given to him by Spirit-anointing. He affirms to us that "I am with you always, to the end of the age." Jesus, whose authority we do not question, is beside us as we engage in the work of making disciples and helping people to live under the rule of God. I have no authority of my own, but I am accompanied on this journey of holiness by the one to whom all authority is committed.

Authority to act

With this encouragement, we might ask ourselves whether we are working on one cause at each of the levels suggested by Charles Elliott. It does not need to be the same cause at each level. At the first level, for example, I could continue to offer food and a warm drink to any beggar I encounter as part of my rule of life. You may want to offer an afternoon a month to help a local family with someone who is housebound. You will certainly be able to think of many other possibilities, and you may already be involved in this kind of work. At the second level, it might be the case that part of your regular giving is to the work of Save the Children or TearFund. The third level is not too hard for those of us who live in a democracy. In the UK it is possible to write to the local Member of Parliament to express concerns about policies which are causing social ills. You can certainly make sure that when they campaign at an election your questions are about those kinds of issues and not about levels of personal tax or other measures which will bring you benefits. Undergirding all of this, of course, is the daily prayer which intercedes for these people and causes.

We have to remember that Jesus was anointed for an authority which came from suffering and not from physical force. Our authority, which flows from his, will have the same source. The picture of Jesus on the cross, crowned with thorns, helps us to see how his authority is not the same as the world's. It flows from his sufferings and it is an authority which is enlarged and made clear in the parody which his captors inflict on him. Earlier in his life he claimed, "And I, when I am lifted up from the earth, will draw all people to myself" (John 12:32), and this has indeed been the case through the subsequent centuries. Without any act of violence on his part, thousands have accepted his rule. Some have so misunderstood the gospel that they have tried to use force to promote it, and we need to apologize to any who have been harmed or violated by such misguided policies. As we contemplate afresh this Lent the humble king who suffered, I believe that this picture holds out the possibility for us to exercise authority as Christians in a way much more in accord with Jesus' example. As a lay person myself, I am continually struck by stories in Christian history which make clear that the suffering and the weak are used by God to exercise an authority which is in excess of anything they might have exercised as part of a stronger, authorized structure. Let's look at some examples.

Browsing in a second-hand bookshop a couple of summers ago, I came across a privately published paperback about a lay woman who had a ministry which was far reaching and extraordinary.[11] Mother Shephard's story is of someone who was brought up in Wales by a devout Christian mother, but who was brought to near suicide by her husband's desertion and the need to bring up three children alone in abject poverty. At the moment when she was about to commit suicide, the Lord miraculously intervened by sending to her someone who was able to make the gospel hope known to her, and she was brought to a saving faith. She became a member of the newly formed Salvation Army. Through her life and witness she brought others to faith from the very neediest people. Then, through her willingness to go wherever General Booth asked, she was at the heart of great movements of revival, in which she suffered a great deal of persecution. Her ministry took her to some dangerous places, but she was willing to go, since she was wholly focused in Jesus. In the story of Mother Shephard we see someone who discovered that the authority of the commissioning Messiah, who accompanied her on her long and distinguished ministry, far outweighed the lack of personal authority she felt as a new convert coming from dismal personal circumstances.

In an earlier century, John Bunyan was equally unwilling to abandon his witness to the gospel and was imprisoned for his disobedience of the local magistrates. In prison he received the dream which he wrote down as *The Pilgrim's Progress*. The influence of his life and writing flowed not from his position in the world, but from suffering and anointing by God for the ministry which he exercised. Like Mother Shephard, John Bunyan was not in the first instance appointed by anyone to change the history of other people –

and yet he did so on the basis of his conviction and his willingness to suffer.

I do not mean that worldly places such as parliaments, police forces and armies lack authority. I do mean, however, that there is a stronger authority in unexpected places – where Christians are living out the gospel in costly self-offering which mirrors the death and resurrection of Jesus Christ. Individuals who trust not in their own power to achieve, but in the power of God, find themselves given authority over sin, over injustice, over death, over evil, over Satan: "For God did not give us a spirit of cowardice, but rather a spirit of power and of love and of self-discipline" (2 Timothy 1:7).

Recently I stood at a checkout counter behind a young man of about fifteen who had three or four glossy car magazines in his hand. Then I heard the worldly-wise twenty-year-old cashier say to him, "Oh, come off it, you can't even drive!" He answered extremely tartly, "I can dream!" Sometimes it seems as if the world (and perhaps the Church) has squashed out of contemporary Western Christians any capacity to dream, envision or hope for anything beyond what we currently experience in our Christian lives. God invites us to dream the big dreams for him, and he longs to anoint us with his Holy Spirit, who will lead us in the dance that will take us into many different and difficult places to establish God's kingdom.

Conclusion

The cross as victory

Some parts of the Christian Church have not found it easy to understand the cross of Jesus in close connection with the resurrection as one single act of salvation. There continues to be a great temptation to maintain that separation as we prepare for Holy Week, over a forty-day period, in a way which can be far more intense than the period after Easter Sunday, when we are offered the chance to celebrate Jesus' coming to life during the fifty days in which we keep the season of Easter! For that reason, it seemed important to reflect on a major theme in the New Testament, that of the cross and resurrection as victory over death, sin and evil. For Jesus, the kingly authority which he exercises in his preaching and healing ministry is not abandoned in death, although we have only scant hints as to how it is exercised during Holy Saturday, before it is restored most gloriously in the resurrection. His reign over God's people is renewed as he is raised to new life, and as he ascends to his Father, to await the end time when he will restore all things to the authority of the Father.

The cross is the place where Jesus "disarmed the rulers and authorities and made a public example of them, triumphing over them in it" (Colossians 2:15). Because he has already triumphed, his disciples can share in that triumph, even in death. In the book of Revelation we read of the martyrs who have entered into that triumph through sharing in a suffering similar to that of Jesus: "Now have come the salvation and the power and the kingdom of our God and the authority of his Messiah, for the accuser of our comrades has been thrown down, who accuses them day and night before our God. But they have conquered him by the blood of the Lamb and by the word of their testimony, for they did not cling to life even in the face of death" (12:10–11).

One of the consequences of which we become aware as we contemplate these things is that Christ's victory is the banner under which we march or the shield under which we shelter. These themes connect with the idea of Christ being above us, which we saw in the words of St Patrick's Breastplate. Whatever is hurled at us in the fight against evil, Christ is above us to protect us, even when we fall or die. It really is the case that those who are marked with the sign of the cross, and who trust in Jesus' death and resurrection as their protection, are awaiting the final victory which they know is his, even while they are in the thick of "mopping-up operations". This is what spiritual warfare is about.

QUESTIONS AND IDEAS

In a group

1 You may wish to pray this litany to the Holy Spirit, which I have written based on the "farewell discourses" of St John's Gospel (found in chapters 14–16).

A litany to the Holy Spirit, "the Helper"

Holy Helper, Spirit of Truth, whom I already know,
Come and be with me for ever.
Father of Jesus, send me the Helper who comes in
    Jesus' name;
I need the Helper who is the Spirit of Truth who
    comes from you.
Holy Helper, come and be with me for ever.
Lord Jesus Christ, send me the Helper from the
    Father, as you have promised me.
Let the Helper teach me everything and be my
    remembrancer of all that you have said to me.
Send the Helper to me, so that he can testify to me
    about you.
Send the Helper to me, so that he can glorify you as
    he abides with me and in me.
Holy Helper, come and be with me for ever.
Holy Spirit, guide me into all truth,
Speak to me whatever you hear,
Declare to me the things that are to come.
Holy Helper, come and be with me for ever.
Prove the world wrong about sin wherever it does not
    believe in you;
Prove the world wrong about righteousness because
    Jesus *has* gone to the Father;
Prove the world wrong about judgment because the
    ruler of this world *has* been condemned.
Holy Helper, Spirit of Truth, whom I already know,
Come and be with me for ever.

THE WOUNDS OF JESUS

2 Review in your group the different stages of
response which your church makes to the needs
of the poor. Are you operating on all levels? If not,
what might you be able to do in your area to make
a difference?

3 Consider how authority is exercised in your
Christian community. Does it mirror the humble
self-giving authority of Jesus? If not, what might
you do to reform it?

By yourself

1 If you find the litany to the Holy Spirit offered
above helpful, then you might think of praying
it as part of your evening prayers – as I do. In my
Anglican tradition, the services of confirmation
and ordination suggest that lay and ordained people
need to be filled daily with the Holy Spirit. A good
time to pray for this renewal is at the end of the
day, when our tiredness reminds us of our need for
God's strength.

2 Reflect on the ways in which you offer friendship
to others. Are there acts of betrayal for which you
need to repent?

3 What is the best you can give to Jesus, or have given
to him? Have you given him anything as costly as
the perfume offered by the woman in the Gospel
story?

4 Do you allow God to partner you in a dance which
enables you to grow in holiness? How could you
follow his lead more closely?

5 Are you entirely focused on Jesus?

Something to pray about

> Christ be above me
> Above my head, as my helmet of salvation
> Christ be above me
> Above my life, as my protection
> Christ be above me
> Above my future, as my banner who leads me on
> Christ be above me
> Above my hopes, as my upward heavenly call
> Christ be above me
> Now and for ever, Amen.

This week you may wish to meditate on, listen to, or sing the following hymns: "Beneath the cross of Jesus I fain would take my stand", and "Oh Sacred Head sore wounded".

FOR FURTHER READING

Raymond Brown, *The Death of the Messiah*, New York: Doubleday, 1994.

Jack Dominic Crossan and Jonathan Reed, *Excavating Jesus*, New York: HarperCollins, 2001.

Charles Elliott, *Comfortable Compassion*, London: Hodder and Stoughton, 1987.

HIS HEART
ASCENSION AND CRUCIFIXION

His body

Human beings are creatures who seem to need, in differing proportions, both novelty and custom. That is true not only in our domestic behaviour, but also in other areas of our lives. Sometimes refreshment comes from taking a walk in a place we have never visited before, while on other occasions it comes from going back to a hilltop or valley which we have explored countless times, because its beauty never fails to refresh or challenge. Sometimes when we cannot visit that place physically, because of illness or distance, we can nevertheless return to it in memory in order to draw strength for current problems, or at least to give us more perspective.

Throughout Christian history, individuals and communities have felt themselves drawn in a similar kind of way to certain aspects of the gospel story, or to characters within the Scriptures, or to features of God himself. These are not the focus to the exclusion of all else, but they are like natural resting places to which people return because they never cease to be a source of inspiration to them.

Perhaps we might keep that in mind as we consider the heart of Jesus, since it might be the case that for many of us this is an unexpected and perhaps curious place on which to focus. If that is the case for you, the invitation is to take the imaginative leap which might enable you to understand; if you find it less alien, there is a chance here to "come home".

A member of a religious community once told me that part of her vocation to the religious life was to worship the heart of Jesus, and so she had tried in the first instance to join a community which was dedicated to the heart of Jesus. Unfortunately, she had a medical condition which meant that the community was not willing to admit her, because their life was so strenuous. Believing that God would have her live a life of prayer, she joined another community whose dedication was closely related but not identical. Now a very old woman, she is still worshipping the Lord Jesus Christ and focusing on his heart of love, within the framework of the community which was willing to receive her. She has lived the life of prayer for many years. The fact that she has been asked by her community to focus more widely than just on the heart of Jesus does not mean that her original vocation has been negated or diminished. Her grace and love evidently flow from his heart of love, which throbbed from conception to crucifixion for the love of others, and which beats now within the heart of God with that same selfless love.

The heart of a person

At the time of Jesus, a person's heart was regarded as the seat of emotions, and a key location of spiritual life, from which worship flowed. Emotions were more openly expressed then than in Western society today, partly because people had no private places. They lived in open communities, and were accustomed to an open way of relating to one another. This is only hinted at in the New

Testament. For instance, Luke records that people wept openly and kissed Paul as he left them to go on to Jerusalem (Acts 20:37). Elsewhere, Paul speaks candidly of his affection for the people he has brought to faith: "For God is my witness, how I long for all of you with the compassion of Christ Jesus" (Philippians 1:8). Such language reveals a real emotional attachment, which many Christians feel towards people with whom they have been able to share the gospel or some significant part of their journey of faith.

Bruce Malina[1] suggests that at the time of Jesus, people predominantly understood themselves in the context of their communities and families, so that individual self-understanding as somehow separate and self-determining in the way that modern Western people now think of themselves was unknown. In this, they were very similar to people in parts of Africa today, where people might say, "I am because we are." Emotional and family attachment was an important part of how people understood themselves and others. This is the essential backcloth against which we need to read the New Testament, which is in stark contrast to our modern individualistic patterns of life, in which we do not share the things on our hearts very easily with one another.

Nevertheless, even in those times, the heart of a person could be hidden, and people recognized that only God knew the human heart (Luke 16:15; Acts 1:24). He is able to search the hearts of people (Romans 8:27), and he tests out their hearts (1 Thessalonians 2:4). The heart was understood to be capable of an immense range of emotions. From the heart of a human being can come both evil thoughts (Mark 7:21) and faith in God (Romans 10:9).

In the case of Jesus, who referred to himself as the Good Shepherd, it is clear that his heart was easily moved with compassion whenever he saw the plight of people who displayed clear needs, such as those who needed healing from blindness: "Moved with compassion, Jesus touched their eyes. Immediately they regained their sight. . ." (Matthew 20:34). Jesus was often emotionally moved by people's circumstances, for he saw the needs which were hidden, noticing the crowds "because they were harassed and helpless, like sheep without a shepherd" (Matthew 9:36).

He wept over sin. As he approached the capital city, Jesus uttered a strong lament at the hardness of heart of those who refused to hear God: "Jerusalem, Jerusalem, the city that kills the prophets and stones those who are sent to it!" Then he revealed his compassionate heart in an amazing picture of motherly tenderness: "How often have I desired to gather your children together as a hen gathers her brood under her wings, and you were not willing!" (Matthew 23:37). We can only imagine the times when, as a child, he had watched a hen scuttling her chicks to safety, which must have been the backcloth to this enormously strong desire of his heart to protect and save those who were his people. I think he may well have felt broken-hearted at the sight of Jerusalem, which was refusing the outstretched hands of God himself, who was offering them new fellowship with him. He was broken-hearted also in foreseeing the eventual outcome for the city at the hands of the Romans, when buildings would be destroyed and the weak and vulnerable would experience desperate suffering (Matthew 24).

Jesus also wept over death – when he finally came to the tomb of his friend Lazarus. Even though he knew he would shortly raise his friend into this life, the encounter with death and bereavement touched his heart and "Jesus began to weep" (John 11:35). Perhaps, like all of us, Jesus was weeping for his own mortality as well as that of Lazarus.

According to the Gospel of John it was the raising of Lazarus that precipitated Jesus' opponents to act to arrest him, so there was the heaviness and smell of death in the air. Thus, while some commented on how much Jesus loved Lazarus, others, seeing the miracle, "went to the Pharisees and told them what he had done". They took serious counsel, thinking, "If we let him go on like this, everyone will come to believe in him, and the Romans will come and destroy both our holy place and our nation" (John 11:48). Ironically, when we put these passages together, we realize that there was safety under the apparently weak wings of the miracle-worker whose hen-like instincts they could not trust; whereas there was no safety in their stratagems against him, so in the end their fears were fulfilled, though not for the reasons that they articulated.

In these stories, we see what Jesus is not: he was not half-hearted, hard-hearted, or soft-hearted. We might sum up the way the Gospel writers speak of Jesus as strong-hearted – his love endures, and warm-hearted – his love flames fiercely for all who need his care.

His wounds

The heart of the crucified

It is hard to imagine what Jesus experienced at his crucifixion. We can be sure, however, that alongside the terrible physical suffering he experienced the emotional anguish of a person dying young and unjustly, as well as the spiritual stress of someone entirely at the mercy of the forces of evil, and yet overwhelmed with the certainty of this being part of the Father's will and the purpose for which he came into the world. No emphasis on the reality of the divine person who is made man in Jesus Christ should underestimate the reality of his human suffering at the hands of those around him. The wounding of his heart was not only physical, as his whole body writhed in agony on the cross, but it was also emotional, as it was pierced by the attitude of others.

Throughout his ministry there had been those who would not listen to him, or who misunderstood him. But there were other more powerful and malicious groups who plotted to bring an end to the popularity of his ministry. This man resorted frequently to the throne of grace in night-time prayer: "In the morning, while it was still very dark, he got up and went out to a deserted place, and there he prayed" (Mark 1:35). After the feeding of the 5,000, he dismissed the crowd and sent the disciples on ahead of him, while "he went up on the mountain to pray" (Mark 6:46). He was accustomed to pouring his heart out to God, his Father, and we can be sure that he carried to him all these bitter encounters with his opponents, in a heart as capable of being wounded by the words and actions of others as yours or mine.

Eventually even his close friends for the most part deserted him (Matthew 26:56), although his heart took some comfort from the women and the beloved disciple, who stayed close throughout the long hours of his crucifixion (John 19:25ff.). "Meanwhile, standing near the cross of Jesus were his mother, and his mother's sister, Mary the wife of Clopas, and Mary Magdalene. When Jesus saw his mother and the disciple whom he loved standing beside her, he said to his mother, 'Woman, here is your son.' Then he said to the disciple, 'Here is your mother.' And from that hour the disciple took her into his own home." Their presence may well have comforted his heart in some way, and his heart was still concerned for them and their future welfare, as his farewell words disclose.

One of the Twelve, to whom he had divulged most clearly the purpose of God's kingdom, ultimately betrayed him. The story of Jesus' consent at the Last Supper to Judas's departure, his acceptance of the kiss (Matthew 26:49) and his refusal to run away from the garden of treachery sometimes lures us into thinking that Jesus did not feel as we know we would feel in circumstances which are in some way comparable. But colleagues who betray confidence by their words or actions do "knock the stuffing" out of a person. We talk of hearts bleeding with sorrow at such times. "Behold, if there is any grief like unto my grief," we cry out.

These afflictions were increased by the denial of the one who had tried to be the most loyal of Jesus' friends. The lies of those who framed him by their false accusations were probably less personally devastating, but nevertheless there was a sting even in them. Public humiliation by the ruler who met and questioned him, and who finally washed his hands of him (Matthew 27:24), was heartbreaking because of that ruler's refusal to adjudicate fairly, and also because this person was choosing not only what to do with a prisoner but also an eternal destiny. The torture of flogging and the ignorant actions of those who pierced him were perhaps easier to bear in his heart than the subsequent scoffing by his countrymen: "And the people stood by, watching; but the leaders scoffed at him, saying, 'He saved others; let him save himself if he is the Messiah of God, his chosen one!' The soldiers also mocked him, coming up and offering him sour wine, and saying, 'If you are the King of the Jews, save yourself!'" (Luke 23:35–37).

The emptying heart of the Son of God

What had prepared the heart of Jesus for this heart-breaking death? The decision of the Son, taken with the Father and the Spirit, to lay aside his majesty in order to become fully human in the womb of Mary began the great demonstration of the nature of God, who is revealed in the self-emptying act of incarnation (Philippians 2). This becomes a theme of Jesus' life, so that at every opportunity of self-aggrandizement or self-preservation, self-emptying remains the way in which he lived. We recall two examples. The first is the temptations, when he was offered the chance to throw himself off the temple and have everyone worshipping him, but he chose to stick with the desert, the searing heat, the desperate hunger and the temptations rather than abandon his God-given call. The second is the foot-washing, when he could have commanded one of his followers to act on his behalf, but he preferred not to hold onto his status and instead offered the service which his companions urgently needed but were not prepared either to request or to offer one another.

This self-emptying is possible because the Son of God knows who he is with the Father and trusts the Father implicitly. What he chooses not to hold for himself, he gives to the Father to keep for him. Status, life and death, the outcome of this risky adventure – all are entrusted not to his own control, but to the providential grace of his heavenly Father.

This is not an exercise in relationship-building between the Father and the Son. That relationship needs no special exercises to strengthen it. Rather, it is all for love of the world. "For God so loved the world," the Gospel writer assures us (John 3:16), and Jesus himself confirms that "I came that they may have life, and have it abundantly" (John 10:10). In order that human beings might not be obliterated, might not lose everything, the Son of God emptied himself, making himself nothing so that we might become sons and daughters of the living God himself. Love is always self-giving, and puts the beloved first. At the moment of incarnation, and in every moment since, the heart of Jesus has been shown to be loving and self-giving.

That heart beats for you and for me. The love of Jesus is for everyone, and it is pure, unconditional love which is offered freely to each person who will receive it. Finding oneself in receipt of such love is not always a comfortable experience. Some cannot bring themselves to believe it. Others cannot entrust themselves to his love. Many think that, although it is offered freely, they had better try to earn it or be worthy of it before they respond. At the Last Supper Peter speaks for many when he protests, "Lord, are you going to wash my feet? . . . You will never wash my feet" (John 13:6, 8). The question is whether we can respond as generously as Peter, who decides to accept all that is on offer. "Lord, not my feet only but also my hands and my head!" In accepting this love and responding in loving gratitude, we begin to comprehend the wounded heart of Jesus; we begin to allow ourselves to be given a new, woundable heart, which can love and give as Jesus did.

His life – ascension and crucifixion

The heart of the ascended one

In other chapters we have looked back at this point in our discussion to see how the wounds of the cross were foreshadowed in the years before the crucifixion, but in this chapter we are looking forward to see how the wounds of Jesus continue beyond the resurrection into eternity.

All the Gospels record the concern in Jesus' heart for the well-being of the disciples when he was on the brink of his arrest and suffering. His love for them was not only for the time they shared together, but also for the time beyond. This theme is picked up by Luke, who records Jesus' concern, as he departed from his disciples for the last time in the days after Easter, that they should not be left desolate. He told them that after waiting in Jerusalem they would receive the promise of the Father. And this "promised one", the Holy Spirit, did come to them, sent by the Son who, in the place of glory, still carried the disciples in his heart of love. This shows beyond doubt that the care Jesus had for his followers throughout his earthly ministry continues beyond the resurrection, for ever.

Jesus carries his disciples in his heart through death and into new resurrection life, which he now enjoys in the ascended glory of his Father. This helps us to understand part of what Paul may mean when he talks of all Christians being "in Christ". The disciples are in his heart, at the right hand of the Father, and their life is hidden with Christ in God (Colossians 3:3). Of course, there is far more to it than this, but we can certainly understand it in that way. In this realm we are acutely aware that we need to use "as if" language, but even so, we can speak of Jesus never appearing before his Father without his disciples, who form part of his body, and to whom he is eternally joined by the Holy Spirit, and who are always in his heart of love. The original handful of followers have been added to by a great multitude of others whom none can number, and who are also in his heart of love. His heart was wounded for them too.

That multitude is still being added to by those who follow Jesus today. As we battle with personal sin and the social wickedness in which we are all implicated, his heart is continually wounded by our failure to live in love, and our failure to allow our personal and social behaviour to flow entirely from our link with him. The love which made him vulnerable in this life keeps him vulnerable to our lives, even in his ascended glory.

He carries us in his heart – by his intercession

We may fairly imagine that the prayers of Jesus during his ministry were not only for himself but also for the disciples who were seeking to follow him. We know that his loving heart prayed for them on the verge of his suffering, and the writer to the Hebrews assures us that what he did then he still does now: "He is able for all time to save those who approach God through him, since he always lives to make intercession for them" (7:25).

It is an ongoing struggle for me to comprehend what it means that the risen and ascended Jesus Christ, whose heart I have wounded by my callousness and wilfulness, nevertheless carries me to the Father's throne of grace continually so that I may be saved and sanctified by his Holy Spirit. I find it hard to hold in balance the importance of the prayers of those around me and my own prayers in the face of his prayer for me, but occasionally I catch a fleeting glimpse of the way that his prayers become their prayers and mine, as the Spirit voices them in us. And in moments of extreme weakness and tiredness, it is good to rest on the prayers of Jesus for me, flowing generously to the Father both despite my wounding of him, but also precisely because of my wounding of him. My hard-heartedness prompts his strong, compassionate heart to prayer, when others wounded by my shortcomings would turn their back on me.

His heart carries the whole world

The care of Jesus Christ extends to the whole world, and is not confined to those who have heard the gospel and responded. His departing words to the disciples in Matthew's Gospel were a command to reach out to everyone: "Go therefore and make disciples of all nations. . ." (28:19). This suggests that the wounds which Jesus bore for love of the whole world indicate in advance that his concern for every person continues for ever. The psalmist's words sum this up: "His steadfast love endures for ever" (136:1). The risen and ascended Jesus has the same heart for the world and the Church as he had in life and on the cross.

What does this mean for us as a faith community?

Knowing the hearts of one another

It is not always possible to understand the heart of other people very easily. This is especially true when they are trying to conceal their heart – when they are bent on evil, for example, or when they do not understand themselves and therefore behave in vastly contradictory ways. Often we only know the public behaviour of a person with whom we work, or the private behaviour of those with whom we live. The possibility of knowing someone "in the round", which might have been feasible in previous generations when people lived very stable lives, in one place, has perhaps gone for ever in the West – except perhaps for those who commit themselves to living in an enclosed religious community.

Only two circumstances come near to that wholeness of perspective. The first is a "case conference", when people from a number of different areas of a person's life meet to piece together painstakingly the whole picture of what this person is doing and may be like. I recently had the opportunity to be part of such a conference, and the outcome might properly have been called a revelation, as each person laid on the table their pieces of the jigsaw in terms of what they had observed. The other circumstance is when a person dies. Again people collaborate to produce an obituary, which makes known not only what was in the public domain already, but also the things which the person may have kept hidden – such as their commitment to some major charitable work, or their unfailing kindness to family and friends, or some major weakness in their character, or a lifelong struggle with a handicap. In these moments we have a little insight into the perspective which the Lord God has on each of us.

Understanding the heart often comes from seeing in the round, although it may also come from a single incident in which the whole is expressed. We may, for instance, hear a radio obituary of a public figure on the day they have died, and that may include some information which makes us revise our hitherto partial view (whether good or bad) of that person. Disclosure of the fuller picture enables a better perspective. On the other hand, a single event can sometimes show us a person's heart in a way which the teeming details of life sometimes mask. I recently had a very significant hour's conversation with a person whose immediate reaction to some news had become something about which she was deeply ashamed. After reflection on that one incident – and our conversation was part of that reflection – she realized that her own heart was not beating as closely to the rhythm of the gospel as she had assumed was the case. Genuine repentance on this occasion enabled her heart to be realigned with the gospel, which was what she desired.

God's hope for human hearts

The gospel is not only about the possibility of forgiveness by God because of the life and death of Jesus Christ, it is also about the possibility of growth in grace throughout our whole lives, so that we are changed from one degree of glory to another (2 Corinthians 3:18). This can only come about as our hearts are changed by the work of God himself, who acts as we invite him to do so, by the power of his Holy Spirit.

This transformation happens as we have a change of heart, which Christians often call repentance, and which can happen as we hear the gospel preached (e.g., Acts 2:37). Using the imagery of the blood and water from the side of Christ, and building on the priestly act of sprinkling the people after a sacrifice as described in the Old Testament, the writer to the Hebrews assures us that, because of Jesus, we can now approach God "in full assurance of faith, with our hearts sprinkled clean from an evil conscience and our bodies washed with pure water" (10:22). We need have no anxieties about whether we are forgiven. When we allow God's gospel word to become part of us, we find that there is a rich harvest. Jesus taught us to expect this: "These . . . when they hear the word, hold it fast in an honest and good heart, and bear fruit with patient endurance" (Luke 8:15). In this and other ways God strengthens our hearts by grace (see Hebrews 13:9).

This secret work of God within us sometimes takes us by surprise, even though others around us have noticed that it is happening. Let me give you a personal example. When I first started teaching, I was driving down a single-track lane when a youth drove far too fast in the other direction and, although I had stopped immediately, he could not stop quickly enough, so I and my passengers sat and watched him drive into us. We were shaken but not hurt. I was furious that he had pranged my nice shiny car, so I got out and explained in very clear terms what I thought about him and his driving. He was so frightened that he begged to be allowed to pay for me to have it mended, and he arrived later that evening with the necessary cash for the repairs. He was obviously more shaken by my wrath than by the accident. I write this with no pleasure, since it was an unreasonable and un-Christian way for me to behave. Some years later, in a busy city, I stopped at some red lights and the elderly driver behind me failed to do the same. Once again I found myself with a dented car. On this occasion, I was personally more shaken since I had not seen him coming at me, but I got out and expressed concern for the elderly man, who was very upset. We exchanged details and, having assured myself that he was not hurt, I drove home. Only later did I realize that, in response to my continued prayer that God would curb my tongue, he had indeed been doing a secret work in my heart which I had not even noticed. This does not mean that I now have perfect control of either my tongue or my temper, but it indicates something of what God can do when we pray that he will soften our hearts.

One way in which this can happen is for us to help one another in the Christian communities in which we live, by encouraging one another when we notice that someone is growing in grace, or by holding one another accountable when we find that the opposite is the case. Many Christians shy away from this, since we are frightened to challenge others, or we feel that we are not perfect ourselves – so how can we talk to others about the ways in which their lives fall short of God's grace? Perhaps this is most easily done when we give one another permission to ask gentle but challenging questions. When people ask me what they should do because they think someone else is engaged in grave sin, I always suggest that they need first to pray regularly that the other person might be given recognition of his or her need for help. Only then can we be ready, when the time comes (and if it falls to us to speak), to open the subject in a way which enables that person to consider the situation before God, and take the necessary action if he or she is indeed outside his good purposes.

This will only happen in a creative way if we are "kind to one another, tender-hearted, forgiving one another, as God in Christ has forgiven you" (Ephesians 4:32). We are encouraged to have "sympathy, love for one another, a tender heart, and a humble mind" (1 Peter 3:8), for we certainly need the forgiveness of others as we also make mistakes and, alas, enter wilfully into sin on occasion. God delights to change hearts when we invite him to do so, therefore we pray often, "Soften our hearts," or, "Enlarge our hearts." Everyday life is an opportunity to grow in love for God and for one another, and this happens as we invite God to be at work in our hearts.

A heart for others in mission

It is clear that the love which Jesus had for people took him to the suffering of a broken heart on the cross, so that all the world might know the Father's love. When we sit at the foot of the cross and see such love, we find that he gives us a love which begins to reflect his own love for others. This leads us into mission to those who have not yet heard of his love.

Many years ago, I went to the Far East for a summer vacation and stayed for a while with a woman who had spent her whole life in a foreign place bringing the gospel to a people whom she evidently loved passionately. I see that same kind of love in the lives of some of the pastors I know who are engaged in planting churches, and in the lives of those who work in many difficult places to bring the practical love of Jesus into the lives of those who cannot hear it, still less believe it, until they have felt it. One of the questions which you might want to consider as a Christian community is how you express something of the love of Jesus to others by faith-sharing. If that is missing entirely from your actions as a community, then one of the things you may want to do as a result of this Lent is to ask others with more experience to show you how to begin.

Theologically we begin with knowing "the love of Christ that surpasses knowledge, so that you may be filled with all the fullness of God" (Ephesians 3:19), because the task of motivating us for mission, guiding us into effective mission and sustaining us in extended mission is all the work of God in and through us. For this reason we have the fullness of God within us. Paul has been talking about how he received the grace of God to complete his vocation to bring to others the good news of "the boundless riches of Christ" (3:8). This is one of the verses to which I often return, because I find it so hard to comprehend that I can be filled with the fullness of God. It seems to be more than I would dare to claim, and certainly more than I would dare to ask, and yet it is there, as clear as can be, not offered but stated, with incredible boldness, as the aim towards which I, with all my sisters and brothers in Christ, am to move. This is about God's loving power, which fills him and is intended to fill us too.

What does this mean for us personally?

Knowing our own heart

Granted that we do not know ourselves as well as we might, I would like to suggest that you spend some time reflecting on your life story in order to see the whole picture in a more conscious way. There are two things upon which it might be helpful to concentrate: (1) periods of life when things were stable, and (2) significant events which changed the way you experienced things. Below, I have started to write my life story in this way so that you can see what I mean. Stable periods are marked *, and significant events are marked #.

Age	Period/Event	Significance
1–7*	Living with my parents and grandparents as the only child in doting but fairly strict group of adults – centre of attention	Felt loved and secure; learned a lot from adults about values
7#	Brother was born; moved to another town with parents	Difficult time adjusting to life without exclusive adult attention
7* (ish)	Discovered reading thanks to new friends	Life transformed forever
11*	Passed the 11+ and won scholarship to independent Christian school	Met people with different cultural backgrounds; imbibed Christian values from Christian school
18#	Failed to be awarded a school honour by head teacher; fellow students gave me a standing ovation at speech day	Broken heart – I had come to love the school very deeply and felt personally devastated as well as amazingly loved

As you create this map of your life, you will perhaps begin to see for the first time in an ordered way some of the things which have gone to making you the person you are, and to shaping your heart. Most of the reflection on the right-hand side of the page will be what you now think about these events, not what you understood or felt at the time. Some things, such as the last event which I have recorded, may be occurrences which have deeply affected your emotions or caused a change of heart. In my case, my deep devotion to the school, which almost amounted to adoration of an unhealthy kind, was broken in one traumatic moment. By the mercy of God, I came to hate neither the school nor the head, but I saw the whole system in a new light – one which was less adulatory and more realistic. Change of heart does not happen often, or easily, and sometimes it needs a trauma to allow the shift to take place.

You may find that the events marked # are the ones which cause you to pause most. Perhaps it would help you to write a little more about these in a separate notebook. When you have finished this task of writing out your life story and making any notes which seem helpful, there are some further things to do. None of this is likely to be done quickly. It is fine to take one Lent to write your life story and another to deal with the emerging issues. Or you could set aside time later in the year, perhaps at Advent. When you are ready, you can begin to reflect a little more on the general trends or specific events in your life. Below are some further things to do.

1 Make a note to yourself about any of the events or trends which you have not consciously brought to God – perhaps mark them with a cross. It may be that some places in your life's journey happened in

such a traumatic way that you have already spent
a good deal of time laying these things before God.
Or the opposite may be the case: they were so very
difficult that God seemed far off and you felt you
had lost contact with the Lord. Or it might be that
some of them happened before you became a
committed Christian, so you have never offered
these events to the Lord specifically. Perhaps this
Lent is an opportunity to spend some time doing
just that. It could be something best done on a quiet
day when you go away from home to pray things
through in a retreat house or house of prayer. Take
your life story with you, and ask God where to
begin. It could be something you decide to do
Sunday by Sunday as you go to worship God with
others. If you belong to a church where you have
Holy Communion every week, then you may want
to make that the intention of your worship and the
issue which you bring to the Lord's table for his
mercy. If you do not think that the main service of
the week will allow you to do that (because there
are too many people around, or too few periods
of silence in the corporate worship), then maybe
an extra time of prayer each week would help.
Or there may be another service of worship each
week in Lent where it would be possible to deal
specifically with these things.

2 If there are some memories which are bitter,
or which have left you with current problems
you know are grounded in the times you have
remembered, then you may need to ask God for
healing. You can do this alone in private prayer,

but you may find it helpful to receive the ministry of healing from other Christians. Many churches offer the ministry of prayer and laying on of hands occasionally, and some offer it very regularly. If you do not know where to receive this, then why not ask other Christians you know whether this is part of their tradition? Most Christian ministers would be willing to pray with you for healing, but do not be upset if you happen to find one who refuses. If the memory is particularly painful or personal, you do not necessarily have to confide in the person who prays with you all the details – God knows them in any case. Just say that you are seeking God's healing of some painful memories, from which you would like to be freed. The memories will probably always be there – but the pain of them should not be. And they certainly should not hamper your growth in love. If they are doing that, then they need God's healing touch.

3 This work may be appropriately followed up by some sharing with other Christians. If you are reading this book as part of a Lent study group which is meeting weekly, then you may wish to spend a meeting sharing on the basis of the life stories you have each written. You will need to give one another permission to share things in absolute confidence, and also allow people to share as little or as much as they wish. If you or your group have never shared in a group before, then maybe a good way to begin would be to encourage one another to share things for which you are now thankful, although at the time you either did not feel

thankful or did not realize that they were positive experiences. To use an illustration from my own life, the experience of finding two friends who went to school with me between the ages of seven and eleven and who were already into reading books – chiefly novels at that stage – was one which I sailed through without really noticing at the time. But now I realize that they gave to me, albeit unconsciously, a gift which has been extremely influential in shaping my life. I have no idea how many books I have read entirely, but they are numbered in thousands. The combination of the loan of books, the habit of borrowing from libraries, and the determination of my parents not to let me read late into the night at this formative stage of my life all produced a heady cocktail which means that reading is now a daily habit of life that neither holidays nor sickness interrupt. It is even influencing the writing of this book. The memory of how influential for good some books have been for me has driven me to pray that this book might be that significant for some who read it. So my retelling of that part of my story would include thankfulness to the family who began the journey, and also to God for the providential combination of factors which gave rise to the habit of reading in my life.

4 In some groups it may be appropriate to share some of the painful things. If you do that, please ensure that it is a group where such things can be handled with respect. You also need to be sure that they are not the kind of memories which are so burdensome that ordinary untrained people might find them

hard to handle. For instance, if one of your memories is of coming home to a break-in where a member of your family was murdered, then it is likely to be most helpful to you (and to your group) for you to seek an ordained person or a qualified counsellor to whom you can talk. Not only may others find your story extremely distressing, but they also may not help you if they do not know how best to react. If as a group you decide that you are ready to share painful things, then please observe these simple guidelines:

- Keep confidences – and do not talk outside the group about this.
- Do not bring the subject up again unless the person concerned asks you to talk about it.
- Pray about what you have heard, and ask God to minister his grace to the person who has shared his or her story.
- Pray about what you have heard, and ask God to minister his grace to you, and especially the grace of forgetfulness for whatever you do not need to remember.

5 It may occasionally be helpful for members of your group to share things which happened in the past, where they now realize that they said or did things that were wrong. They may only have come to realize this recently, or it may be something which they have had a bad conscience about for months or even years. If that is the case, then you need to add the following to the guidelines above:

- If people recount something which they think was wrong, and they are wanting to repent and put it right, then do not try to make them feel better about it by making light of what they have shared. It may or may not be what the world counts as a grave sin, but when the Holy Spirit moves people to recognize things that were wrong in the past, the best help we can offer is to assure them of God's forgiveness in Jesus Christ, and of our prayers as they seek to live in a different way in the future.

- Remember that all have sinned and fallen short of the glory of God – so do not allow yourself to gloat over the sins of others. Pray for real humility which mourns over your own sins as well as over the sins of others.
- If your church tradition is either to make confession to a minister/priest or to make public confession/testimony in a service of worship, then encourage the person concerned also to observe that tradition.

Conclusion

Costliness

Whichever of the wounds of Jesus we may contemplate, we will be struck by the costliness of our redemption. Although we cannot comprehend this fully, it is a theme which is offered to us as a way of helping us to understand what Jesus has done for us. Peter puts it like this: "You know that you were ransomed from the futile ways inherited from your ancestors, not with perishable things like silver or gold, but with the precious blood of Christ, like that of a lamb without defect or blemish" (1 Peter 1:18–19).

acknowledge that he leads us into suffering: "For he has graciously granted you the privilege not only of believing in Christ, but of suffering for him as well – since you are having the same struggle that you saw I had and now hear that I still have" (Philippians 1:29–30). Keeping Christ's costly woundedness before us enables us to learn how to suffer, and to receive that suffering as a privilege of God's grace.

This suffering, of course, is for the sake of the gospel. It is not the suffering of a victim who is subject to repeated illegal or immoral acts on the part of those who wickedly use their power over the weaker party. There is a world of difference between a woman who suffers physical pain and deprivation because she has chosen to go to share the love of Christ in a poor part of the world, and the suffering of a prostitute at the hands of her pimp. The first is voluntary, the second involuntary. The first is redemptive, the second exploitative. The death of Jesus cannot and should not be used as a warrant for all kinds of suffering. The fact that he protested at injustice against the weak demonstrates that he does not call the weak to suffer more injustice, but rather calls the strong to suffer in order to protect the weak.

It is hard to know how to explain this, since it can sound like a cranky delight in pain, whereas it is really a joy which knows no comparison to deny ourselves for Jesus' sake, for the sake of the gospel or his little ones. We only need to think of those who give their whole lives in the service of others. Perhaps they work in a drug rehabilitation centre, or nurse the victims of AIDS, or bring relief to the starving of the world. They may work away from home, close to the pain of those who suffer, and often without the financial rewards which are available to those who work in less threatening environments. Yet Christians who work in these and other self-sacrificing ways will tell you that the hard work and suffering which they endure is far outweighed by seeing God's hand at work, and by the sheer joy of being able to minister the grace and love of Jesus to others. In this, they surely help us to see that the wounds of Jesus were also his joy, as well as his glory, since they are the means whereby the freedom of slaves is guaranteed.

QUESTIONS AND IDEAS

In a group

1 Ask one of the group to read Matthew 23:37–39 slowly and with good pauses, so that everyone can enter into the narrative imaginatively. Consider which cities you want to weep over, and then what your hopes for those cities are. How might you pray for them? What might you do for them?

2 Discuss together the specific suggestion as to how you might be "kind-hearted to one another" so that you can help one another. In particular, consider whether the group is ready for any kind of sharing, and at what level. When you are all agreed, then you can begin the process of actually sharing.

3 Tell one another about how hot or cold your hearts are for mission. Try to be honest about why you feel as you do. Consider what you might be able to do together. Do you need to ask someone to come to talk to you about this, or can you learn from one another about ways to serve others and to share your faith with them?

4 Pray the following litany together:

Merciful Lord, fill our hearts with love for you:
Keep our eyes on you, the Christ before us.
Merciful Lord, fill our hearts with love for you:
Remind us of the cost of our redemption.
Merciful Lord, fill our hearts with love for you:
Give us a heart which loves your people.
Merciful Lord, fill our hearts with love for you:
Give us a humble heart which can receive your love.

Merciful Lord, fill our hearts with love for you:
Show us your own heart, wounded with love for us.
Merciful Lord, fill our hearts with love for you:
Keep us in your heart, ascended in the presence of
    your Father.
Merciful Lord, fill our hearts with love for you:
For your love and mercy's sake, Amen.

5 Pray together for any people close to you who
do not yet know or understand the love of the
wounded heart of Jesus for them.

By yourself

1 In addition to the specific ideas which I have given
you beginning on page 206, you may wish to ask
God which facet of the Christian faith is the "heart"
of your devotion, to which you should return
regularly for refreshment.

2 Consider whether you are willingly receiving the
love of Jesus. If not, ask yourself what is stopping
you being open to receive from him. When you are
given the answer, ask God to remove any blockages
which he has revealed to you.

3 Ask God to show you whether your heart beats in
tune with the gospel, as he desires for you.

4 Pray that God will soften your heart.

A prayer for this week

Thanks be to thee,
O Lord Christ,
for all the benefits which thou hast given us;
for all the pains and insults which thou hast borne for us.

O merciful Redeemer,
friend,
and brother,
may we know thee more clearly,
love thee more dearly,
and follow thee more nearly;
for thine own sake, Amen.[2]

FOR FURTHER READING

Bruce J. Malina, *The New Testament World*, Louisville, KY:
WJK Press, 2001.

Conclusion

About forty days ago, we began our consideration of Jesus' wounds, and this conclusion enables us to draw together some of the themes we have explored. I have not tried to give an exhaustive account of the meaning of the death of Jesus, but have only tried to approach it from a fresh angle. First, however, we need to complete the picture.

The burial and the wounds

Josephus suggests that Jews were most careful to remove bodies from the cross for burial, since they hated the Roman practice of leaving them exposed. Usually they were not given honourable burial, but were put in a tomb prepared for such felons, although once decomposed the bones were sometimes deposited in the family grave. As a member of the council, Joseph of Arimathea could well have had access to the tombs that were ready at all times for people executed in this way.

It seems that criminals were normally crucified naked, but the story of the casting of dice for Jesus' cloak suggests that the Romans may have made concessions to the Jewish horror of nakedness, so we must assume that Jesus was reclothed after the flogging and the mocking in the purple cloak. This is certainly what Christian art supposes when it depicts Jesus on the cross wearing a loincloth. But we have to remember that his body would have been an utter mess by the time Pilate gave leave for him to be taken down from the cross. Joseph of Arimathea, if he was indeed a secret sympathizer with "the Way", would probably have wanted to cover the ugly scars gently before laying Jesus' body in the tomb, so they observed as much of the burial rites as time and approaching dark would allow.

John's Gospel suggests that Joseph was indeed a covert disciple of Jesus. If so, he was taking a significant risk in getting involved with the burial, because he could be thought by his own people to be collaborating with Jesus' followers, or by Rome to be associated with treason. On the other hand, if he was part of the Sanhedrin, even if he was absent on that fateful Thursday night when it agreed to send Jesus to Pilate for crucifixion, then he might have been in a less dangerous situation and could perhaps genuinely claim that he was taking such action simply to fulfil the law.[1] We could suppose he regarded that as more important than maintaining his own ritual purity, which was surrendered as soon as he touched the body of Jesus. If Joseph was not known to be a disciple, then that would explain why the women did not help him, but stood at a distance and watched, intending to come back later. And thus the lacerated and scarred body of the Saviour was delivered into Joseph's arms.

The resurrection and the wounds

On Sunday, when the women went to the tomb to anoint the body, they expected to find the stone rolled across to close the entrance, and they remembered rather too late that they would need help to shift it. In fact, as we know, the body was no longer there, for Jesus had risen and was waiting to meet Mary Magdalene before appearing to the other disciples. Their fear and joy knew no bounds, although the latter soon drove out the former. Every aspect of their faith and life then needed to be rethought. One of the key reasons why they were convinced that the person whom they met on a number of occasions was really Jesus was that his body had the marks of the wounds which identified the risen Jesus as identical with the crucified Jesus – albeit in a glorified and transformed body, no longer limited by space and time.

After the dejected couple on the road to Emmaus had rushed back to Jerusalem to tell the other disciples that they had walked, talked and eaten with Jesus, he appeared to the disciples. His greeting was "Peace be among you", but his presence was fear within them. As I write, my parents have been suddenly bereaved, and I know from their reactions that nerves are jangling with shock and disbelief at a most unlooked-for death which has deeply disturbed them. It happens to everyone at these moments, so we should not be surprised that the disciples reacted so badly. What *was* this apparition before them? What were they to make of it? Their frame of reference did not offer them a fourth alternative to "cold dead", ghostly presence, or imposter.

It was this same stark alternative which contributed to my own conversion while I was a teenager. I was very familiar with the Christian story, but I had not made any adult or personal commitment to follow Jesus. Indeed, I had rather tried to avoid it when I was prepared for confirmation! On the Easter morning when I went to take my first Communion, a young preacher asked, "How many people do you know who have risen from the dead?" With the arrogance of youth, I responded in my heart, "None. People don't rise from the dead!" At that moment I realized that I had spoken my deepest belief, and that I neither believed in Jesus risen, nor knew him as the living Lord myself. For some weeks I struggled with this unwelcome recognition, until I was unwittingly challenged by a contemporary. I went on to think and pray, until I could answer the original question, "How many people do you know who have risen from the dead?" with the answer, "One: the Lord Jesus Christ!" I hope this glimpse of my life story may help you to think through your own commitment and faith in Jesus risen, and you may wish to pause here to do your own thinking and praying.

The first disciples found themselves convinced that this was no "cold dead" person, for he was standing before them. They then became convinced that this was no imposter, for he offered to show them his hands and his feet. And they were finally convinced that this was no ghost either, by Jesus' offer to identify himself to them in eating broiled fish. None of these "signs" were sufficient in themselves to identify the reality of the risen Jesus, but the combination was utterly convincing. The recognition of him as the person who had walked and talked with them through three outstanding years, the sight of his wounds and his willingness to eat with them as he always had done all added up to an unprecedented outcome, which they had not anticipated despite the preparation Jesus had offered them in his teaching before his death.

His wounds and our wounds

One of the consequences of meeting with the risen Lord who had been crucified was that the attitude of the disciples towards death changed completely. First, they found that they were able to respond to Jesus' call to take up the cross and follow him daily, by the power of the Holy Spirit whom he breathed on them, and who came to them in a remarkable way soon after he left them for the final time. Secondly, they found that they were bold in the face of opposition and persecution in the way Jesus had shown when faced with similar trials. As his daily carrying of the cross had prepared him to suffer death, so their daily carrying of the cross also prepared them for suffering. Thirdly, they were ready for persecution and death because they now knew that death was not the end and was therefore not to be feared. Jesus' resurrection had shown them that they too could hope for resurrection from the dead. They no longer feared those who could harm the body, since they knew that Jesus had secured their eternal salvation. His wounds for them, now glorified in resurrection and ascension, strengthened them in the face of situations which brought them similar wounds. And that has been the experience of the Church ever since.

During 2000, I was fortunate to be asked by the Archbishop of Canterbury to represent the Anglican Communion at the Roman Catholic international conference of lay people in Rome, to celebrate the millennium. It was a wonderful opportunity to hear how the Church worked in so many different parts of the world, but there were also opportunities for those present to worship and open themselves to God for renewal. The most memorable of those services for me took place on a Sunday afternoon in the catacombs. On simple benches, where Christians in the very first days had worshipped and prayed for those who were being martyred, we heard story after story from every part of the world of Christians who had carried their cross to martyrdom in the twentieth century. For every person described, a candle was lit to commemorate a life which had burned brightly for Christ.

At the end of a long afternoon we were facing a sea of candles, and were reminded that we "are surrounded by so great a cloud of witnesses". For me, it was not hard to be asked to "lay aside every weight and the sin that clings so closely", so that we can "run with perseverance the race that is set before us, looking to Jesus the pioneer and perfecter of our faith, who for the sake of the joy that was set before him endured the cross, disregarding its shame, and has taken his seat at the right hand of the throne of God" (Hebrews 12:1–2). Hearing just a few of the stories of Christians who had carried their cross and endured the wounds which were their martyrdom, and reflecting on the thousands who had suffered – more in the twentieth century than any other – was inspiration enough for a lifetime.

The wounds and our worship

The wounded and crucified Jesus, now risen and ascended, carries his wounds into the presence of the Father. His first role there is to plead for us his death on the cross of which his wounds are the permanent reminder. Of all the books in the New Testament, the one which is most aware of the glorified yet wounded Saviour is the one which is also most full of adoration and worship, and that is the book of Revelation. The heavenly worship recorded in its pages has inspired some of our most beautiful hymns and songs of worship. Although it is a complex book, with many themes interwoven, it is a book of worship to Jesus as the Lamb of God. If you have a Bible in which the poetry is set out in verse form, you will see that scattered through the text are songs of adoration in which the author joins the choirs of heaven in expressing love and praise. One such example may be found in Revelation 5:6–14.

Many of these hymns focus on the suffering of Jesus, his death, his blood and his victory. As well as songs of praise, there are great invitations to worship. Twice the writer of the visions is encouraged to "worship God" when it seems as though he is about to bow down to another heavenly servant of God (19:10; 22:9). And the worship of the glorified yet wounded Lord Jesus is closely associated with the worship of God himself. In pictorial terms, we "see" the unity of the Father with the Son before a fully worked-out trinitarian theology has been articulated. So, "To the one seated on the throne and to the Lamb, be blessing and honour and glory and might for ever and ever!" (5:13). In graphic terms, we are invited to share in the life of God himself. "The faithful and true witness" (3:14), who is identified as Jesus himself, says, "To the one who conquers I will give a place with me on my throne, just as I myself conquered and sat down with my Father on his throne" (3:21).

The sovereignty of the Father in which the Son shares is also shared with those who trust in him. This means that in facing up to evil and combating injustice, the victory of Jesus which is already assured is coming on earth as in heaven. When we bring the name of Jesus to combat evil in prayer or in ministry, or when we appeal to his wounds and his shed blood, the evil one cannot resist. We know that Jesus has the victory and there is no one and nothing which can withstand him. At these moments, in which we experience an anticipation of the end-time victory of Jesus over all that opposes God's righteous rule, we find ourselves exulting in the Spirit as our hearts are full of wonder and praise at the grace and mercy of Jesus, wounded for us.

His wounds and the wounds
of our sisters and brothers in Christ

Although the suffering of Jesus in the last week of his life is over, we cannot forget that our fellow brothers and sisters, who are part of his body, still face persecution for their faith and that for his sake they carry their wounds, which in a real sense are his wounds too. We cannot always know what is happening in lands where the Christian faith is forbidden and the Church is underground. Nor can we always intervene to prevent physical torture, although where it is possible to protest we should certainly do so. But we can ensure that we are regular in our prayer for the suffering Church, so that they (and we) may be given courage to hold the faith.

When I meet Christians from the churches overseas where there is or has been physical suffering for their faith, I find that I can begin to engage in a new way with the question of what the wounds of Christ mean. For them his wounds have not been their physical protection, but his Holy Spirit has enabled them to carry the wounds of the crucified with dignity and love and, most importantly, without resentment. Two people I met in South Africa picture that for me. One whose woundedness was very evident physically was nevertheless living life as fully as possible in a very matter-of-fact way. He was still following Jesus, despite severe handicap. Another, a priest, whose wounds were invisible to the casual acquaintance, had nevertheless suffered in an equally severe way for his faith. Their dignified persistence helps me to pray for others whom I do not know, but whose lifelong pain or current suffering at the hands of persecuters could bring bitterness. For them I pray for special grace.

The life, death and resurrection of Jesus has restored our broken relationship with God and enabled us to receive God himself, in the Holy Spirit, into our lives so that the relationship can be maintained for ever. We call this process of being put into right relationship with God justification and sanctification, which flow from the cross of Jesus the wounded one. Our part in the process is to believe in him, and to receive his forgiveness.

For many Christians, what is offered to us by the outstretched hands of Jesus on the cross is simply too familiar for us to appreciate its enormity. But I remember explaining this free gift of grace to a class of thirteen-year-old boys when I first started teaching. One spoke for all: "You mean that you get off, scot-free? Even *you*, Miss?" His tone conveyed fury at the thought of this injustice. He had grasped the parable of the equal wages for all labourers in one moment. The generous gift of new relationship with God *is* offered to all who will receive it. Jesus "was wounded for our transgressions", and our response is rightly thanks and praise, which we offer not only with our lips but in our lives. In the Introduction I wrote about offering our whole life as a sacrifice of joy to the one who has offered all for us. On the eve of Easter, we may want to consider how we can more fittingly make that offering to the wounded Jesus who is our risen Lord.

A prayer for Holy Week

Almighty God and Father, your beloved Son willingly
endured the agony and shame of the cross for our
redemption. Give us the courage to take up our cross
and follow him in newness of life and hope. He lives and
reigns with you and the Holy Spirit, one God now and
for ever. Amen.[2]

NOTES

Introduction

1 G.S. Loyan, *The Crucifixion of Jesus: History, Myth, Faith*, Minneapolis: Augsburg Fortress Press, 1995, p. 171.

Chapter 1. His Back

1 R. Brown, *The Death of the Messiah*, New York: Doubleday, 1994, p. 913.

2 If you wish to read more about this, then see Russ Parker's book *Healing Wounded History*.

Chapter 2. His Feet

1 A.C. Bouquet, *Everyday Life in New Testament Times*, London: Batsford, 1954, p. 65.

2 K.C. Hanson and D.E. Oakman, *Palestine in the Time of Jesus*, Minneapolis: Augsburg Fortress Press, 1998, p. 93.

3 J.D. Crossan and J.L. Reed, *Excavating Jesus*, New York: HarperCollins, 2001, p. 3.

4 I have been helped in thinking about this section by J.B. Gibson, *The Temptations of Jesus in Early Christianity*, and by J. H. Yoder, *The Politics of Jesus*, although I have not adopted all of their conclusions, and in the matters relating to the last hours of Jesus' life have adopted a fresh approach.

5 This is the suggestion of J.B. Gibson.

6 If you are wondering about the feeding of the 5,000 and the miracles, I think these were done out of compassion and in no way as an attempt to demonstrate his identity.

7 R. Brown, *The Death of the Messiah*, New York: Doubleday, 1994, pp. 573–86.

8 Although I am not following the thesis at every point, I have been much helped in my thinking about this matter by the work of John Christopher Thomas.

9 Bruce J. Malina, *Windows on the World of Jesus*, Louisville, KY: WJK Press, 1993, p. 40.

10 The title of a book by Helder Camara.

11 *The Book of Alternative Services of the Anglican Church of Canada*, Toronto: Anglican Book Centre, 1985, pp. 512–13.

Chapter 3. His Hands

1 J.D. Crossan and J.L. Reed, *Excavating Jesus*, London: SPCK, 2001, p. 32.

2 Ibid., p. 33.

3 Ibid., pp. 15–50. I am chiefly indebted to this research for the whole of this section.

4 M. Sawicki, *Crossing Galilee*, Harrisburg, PA: Trinity Press, 2000, p. 17.

5 Crossan and Reed, p. 21, citing Eusebius, *Ecclesiastical History*, 3.20 (italics mine).

6 B.W. Harrison, "The Power of Anger in the Work of Love", *Union Seminary Quarterly Review* 36 (1981): p. 49.

7 He has already spelled it out at Caesarea Philippi (Mark 8:31–33).

8 *SPCK Book of Prayers*, London: SPCK, 1995, p. 66.

Chapter 4. His Side

1 B.J. Malina, *Windows on the World of Jesus*, Louisville, KY: WJK Press, 1993, pp. 33–34.

2 Malina, *The New Testament World*, Louisville, KY: WJK Press, 2001, p. 82.

3 Ibid.

4 R. Brown, *The Death of the Messiah*, New York: Doubleday, 1994, p. 1177.

5 Ibid., p. 1178.

6 D. Dyas (ed.), *Images of Salvation: The Story of the Bible through Medieval Art*, Christianity and Culture, St John's Nottingham and the University of York, 2004. It may be ordered through www.stjohns-nottm.ac.uk.

7 Jim Bishop in *The Day Christ Died* suggests: ". . .the spear drove inwards between the fifth and sixth ribs. It went through the pleura and the thin part of the lungs and stopped in the pericardium. The dead do not bleed ordinarily but the right auricle of the human heart holds liquid blood after death and the outer sac holds a serum called hydro-pericardium." After the weapon had been withdrawn, these fluids ran out of the side of Jesus and were recorded by the writer of the fourth Gospel. But this is not undisputed.

8 See A. Heron, *Tale and Tradition*, Edinburgh: Handsel Press, 1983, p. 164. Heron suggests that it is like a piece of metal which is "trans-signified" into a coin while remaining the same piece of metal. What happens is that its meaning is different and it is treated differently. Something similar happens when we set aside bread and wine to remember Jesus.

9 Attributed to St Patrick (*c*.389–461), this version by Cecil Frances Alexander (1818–95), in Wesley Milgate (ed.), *With One Voice*, London: Collins, 1979, no. 454.

10 Augustus Toplady (1740–78), cited in The Standing Committee of the General Synod of the Church of Ireland

(ed.), *Church Hymnal*, Oxford: Oxford University Press, 2000, no. 557.

11 David L. Fleming, *Draw Me Into Your Friendship*, St Louis, MO: Institute of Jesuit Sources, 1996, p. 2.

12 We do not have the original text of any New Testament document – only handwritten copies, which do not always agree. Usually mistakes can be spotted, but it is not always clear which is nearest to the autograph copy. The science of examining this is called textual criticism.

13 See especially Hebrews 5:7–9; 9:14; 10:5–14.

14 A. Lincoln, *Ephesians*, World Biblical Commentary, Dallas: Word, 1990, p. 312.

Chapter 5. His Head

1 J.D. Crossan and J.L. Reed, *Excavating Jesus*, London: SPCK, 2001, pp. 23–27.

2 R. Brown, *The Death of the Messiah*, New York: Doubleday, 1994, p. 255.

3 Ibid.

4 Ibid., p. 865ff.

5 Ibid., p. 963.

6 Ibid., p. 1063.

7 K. Barth, *Church Dogmatics*, IV, 2, Edinburgh: T & T Clark, 1958, p. 788.

8 D. Nineham, *St Mark*, Rickmansworth: Penguin, 1963, p. 372.

9 Barth, *Church Dogmatics*, p. 797.

10 C. Elliott, *Comfortable Compassion*, London: Hodder and Stoughton, 1987.

11 C. Preece, *Woman of the Valleys: The Story of Mother Shepherd*, Port Talbot: New Life Publications, 1988.

Chapter 6. His Heart

1 B.J. Malina, *The New Testament World*, Louisville, KY: WJK Press, 2001, pp. 58–80.
2 Richard of Chichester (1197–1253) in *The SPCK Book of Christian Prayer*, London: SPCK, 1995, p. 66.

Conclusion

1 See Deuteronomy 21:22–23.
2 *The Book of Alternative Services of the Anglican Church of Cancada*, Toronto: Anglican Book Centre, 1985, p. 131.

We want to hear from you. Please send your comments about this book to us in care of zreview@zondervan.com. Thank you.

GRAND RAPIDS, MICHIGAN 49530 USA

WWW.ZONDERVAN.COM